LET'S LEARN JAPANESE
IV

LET'S LEARN JAPANESE
IV

Nobuko Mizutani

NHK Overseas Broadcasting Department

KODANSHA INTERNATIONAL
Tokyo • New York • London

Concept and dialogues: Nobuko Mizutani
Accompanying notes and drills: Michiko Hongo
Producer for radio: Takeshi Sakurai
Assistant Producer: Takehito Kobayashi
Director: Hiroshi Shioguchi
Dialogue Readers: Masatoshi Kawada (Instructor)
and Miyoko Goto (Model Speaker)
Sound effects: Hirokatsu Takemura

Note: The lessons in this book are available on audio cassette in bookstores or from the publisher.

The text of this book is based entirely on the broadcasts of Radio Japan's *Let's Learn Japanese* series. For further information about these broadcasts, including schedules and frequencies, please write directly to the following address:

> *Let's Learn Japanese*
> Radio Japan, NHK
> Tokyo 150-01
> Japan

Distributed in the United States by Kodansha America, Inc., 114 Fifth Avenue, New York, N.Y. 10011, and in the United Kingdom and continental Europe by Kodansha Europe Ltd., 95 Aldwych, London WC2B 4JF. Published by Kodansha International Ltd., 17-14 Otowa 1-chome, Bunkyo-ku, Tokyo 112, and Kodansha America, Inc. Copyright © 1994 by NHK. All rights reserved. Printed in Japan.

ISBN 4-7700-1788-X

First edition, 1994

94 95 96 97 98   10 9 8 7 6 5 4 3 2 1

CONTENTS

NOTE

This volume is a continuation of
LET'S LEARN JAPANESE I, II, and III.
A description of romanization, special symbols, etc.
appears in the introduction to the first volume.

AꞋRASHIYAMA O MINAꞋGARA
嵐山を見ながら
In Arashiyama

	Today's Conversation
Yamamoto.	**KaꞋwa no mukoꞋo wa AꞋrashiyama to yuuꞋ yaꞋmaꞋ desu.** 川のむこうは嵐山という山です。 The mountain across the river is called Arashi-yama.
Smith:	**KiꞋ ga taꞋkusan aꞋtte, kiꞋree na yaꞋmaꞋ desu ne.** 木がたくさんあって、きれいな山ですね。 It's a beautiful mountain with lots of green trees, isn't it?
Yamamoto:	**EꞋe, koꞋno hen waꞋ saꞋkura no meeshoꞋ de, haꞋru wa haꞋnami no hitoꞋ de iꞋppai ni naꞋru soo desu.** ええ、このへんは桜の名所で、春は花見の人でいっぱいになるそうです。 Yes. This area is famous for its cherry blossoms. They say that it is full of cherry-blossom viewers in the spring.
Smith:	**SoꞋo desu ka.** そうですか。 Is that right?
Yamamoto:	**DoꞋko ka de shaꞋshin o torimashoꞋo.** どこかで写真をとりましょう。 Shall we take a picture?

Smith:	A⌈no hashi no ue⌉ wa ⌈do⌉o desu ka. あの橋の上はどうですか。 What about on the bridge?
Yamamoto:	I⌉i desu ne. So⌉rosoro ku⌈raku na⌉tte kimashita kara, i⌈sogimasho⌉o. いいですね。そろそろ暗くなってきましたから、いそぎましょう。 Good. Let's hurry, since it is getting dark.

ARASHIYAMA O MINAGARA
嵐山を見ながら
In Arashiyama

Kawa: Today, in Lesson 40, Mr. Smith and Mr. Yamamoto visit Arashiyama, a scenic mountain famous for its cherry blossoms. Our first key sentence is, "There's a mountain across the river."

Goto: **Ka⌈wa no muko⌉o ni ya⌈ma⌉ ga arimasu.**
川のむこうに山があります。

Kawa: "There's a mountain," **yama ga arimasu; yama** means "a mountain;" "across the river," **kawa no mukoo ni**; "river" is **kawa.** So, "There's a mountain across the river."

Goto: **Ka⌈wa no muko⌉o ni ya⌈ma⌉ ga arimasu.**
川のむこうに山があります。

Kawa: Now, substitutions. "There's the sea across the mountain." "The sea" is **umi.**

Goto: **Ya⌈ma no muko⌉o ni ⌈u⌉mi ga arimasu.**
山のむこうに海があります。

Kawa: Next, "There's a bank across the road." "Road" is **michi** and "bank," **ginkoo.**

Goto: **Mi⌈chi no muko⌉o ni gi⌈nkoo ga arima⌉su.**
道のむこうに銀行があります。

Kawa: Our second key sentence is, "It has become a little dark."

Goto: **Su⌈ko⌉shi ku⌈raku narima⌉shita.** 少し暗くなりました。

Kawa: Here, we practice **narimashita**, something "has become" some way. "A little dark" is **sukoshi kuraku.** "It has become a little dark."

Goto: **Su⌈ko⌉shi ku⌈raku narima⌉shita.** 少し暗くなりました。

Kawa: Let's say "a little bright," **sukoshi akaruku.** "It has become a little bright."

Goto: **Su⌐ko⌐shi a⌐karuku narima⌐shita.**　少し明るくなりました。

Kawa: Next, we practice "a little quiet," **sukoshi shizuka ni.** "It has become a little quiet."

Goto: **Su⌐ko⌐shi ⌐shi⌐zuka ni narimashita.**　少し静かになりました。

Kawa: Now we deal with our third key sentence, "It's beginning to get dark, isn't it?" It's slightly different from "It has become dark." **Kuraku narimashita.** Listen first.

Goto: **So⌐rosoro ku⌐raku na⌐tte ki⌐ma⌐shita ne.**
そろそろ暗くなってきましたね。

Kawa: "It's beginning to get dark, isn't it?" **Soro-soro** itself means "slowly," "by slow degrees," "little by little." **Kuraku natte** is the -te form of **kuraku narimasu,** followed by **kimashita—kuraku natte kimashita,"** the whole phrase meaning practically "is beginning to get dark." The last **ne** means "isn't it?" "It's beginning to get dark, isn't it?"

Goto: **So⌐rosoro ku⌐raku na⌐tte ki⌐ma⌐shita ne.**
そろそろ暗くなってきましたね。

Kawa: How about the weather getting worse? "Weather" is **tenki.** "The weather's getting worse." **Tenki ga waruku natte kimashita.** "The weather's gradually getting worse, isn't it?"

Goto: **So⌐rosoro ⌐te⌐nki ga ⌐wa⌐ruku natte ki⌐ma⌐shita ne.**
そろそろ天気が悪くなってきましたね。

♪ **Station Break** ⸺⸺⸺⸺⸺⸺⸺⸺⸺⸺⸺⸺⸺⸺

Kawa: Now, in the second half of this session, we'll discuss each dialogue. Listen to their conversation first.

◆ **Today's Conversation**

Y: **Ka⌐wa no muko⌐o wa A⌐rashiyama to yuu⌐ ya⌐ma⌐ desu.**
川のむこうは嵐山という山です。

S: **Ki⌐ ga ta⌐kusan a⌐tte, ki⌐ree na ya⌐ma⌐ desu ne.**
木がたくさんあって、きれいな山ですね。

Y: **E⌐e, ko⌐no hen wa⌐ sa⌐kura no meesho⌐ de, ha⌐ru wa ha⌐nami no hito⌐ de i⌐ppai ni na⌐ru soo desu.**
ええ、このへんは桜の名所で、春は花見の人でいっぱいになるそうです。

S: **So⌐o desu ka.**　そうですか。

Y: **Do⌐ko ka de sha⌐shin o torimasho⌐o.**
どこかで写真をとりましょう。

S: **A⌐no hashi no ue⌐ wa ⌐do⌐o desu ka.**　あの橋の上はどうですか。

Y: I⌐i desu ne. So⌐rosoro ku⌐raku na⌐tte kimashita kara, i⌐sogimashoo.
いいですね。そろそろ暗くなってきましたから、いそぎましょう。

Kawa: Next, you'll listen to its English version.

◆ **Same Conversation in English**

Y: The mountain across the river is called Arashiyama.

S: It's a beautiful mountain with lots of green trees, isn't it?

Y: Yes. This area is famous for its cherry blossoms. They say that it is full of cherry-blossom viewers in the spring.

S: Is that right?

Y: Shall we take a picture?

S: What about on the bridge?

Y: Good. Let's hurry, since it is getting dark.

Kawa: Now each dialogue. We start with Mr. Yamamoto's remark, "The mountain across the river is called Arashiyama."

Goto: **Ka⌐wa no muko⌐o wa A⌐rashiyama to yuu⌐ ya⌐ma⌐ desu.**
川のむこうは嵐山という山です。

Kawa: You remember the first key sentence. **Kawa no mukoo** means "across the river." **Arashiyama to yuu yama,** "a mountain called Arashiyama. "A mountain across the river is called Arashiyama."

Goto: **Ka⌐wa no muko⌐o wa A⌐rashiyama to yuu⌐ ya⌐ma⌐ desu.**
川のむこうは嵐山という山です。

Kawa: Mr. Smith responds, "It's a beautiful mountain with lots of trees, isn't it?"

Goto: **Ki⌐ ga ta⌐kusan a⌐tte, ki⌐ree na ya⌐ma⌐ desu ne.**
木 がたくさんあって、きれいな山ですね。

Kawa: This literally reads as **ki ga takusan atte,** "there are lots of trees, and...," **kiree na yama desu ne,** "it's a beautiful mountain, isn't it?" Mr. Yamamoto explains. "Yes. This area is famous for its cherry blossoms. They say that it is full of cherry-blossom viewers in the spring."

Goto: **E⌐e, ko⌐no hen wa⌐ sa⌐kura no meesho⌐ de, ha⌐ru wa ha⌐nami no hito⌐ de i⌐ppai ni na⌐ru soo desu.**
ええ、このへんは桜の名所で、春は花見の人でいっぱいになるそうです。

Kawa: Let's break this into two. "Yes. This area is famous for its cherry blossoms." "This area," **kono hen;** "cherry blossoms," **sakura; meesho** means a "famous place." "Yes. This area is famous for its cherry blossoms, and..."

Goto: **E⌐e, ko⌐no hen wa⌐ sa⌐kura no meesho⌐ de,**
ええ、このへんは桜の名所で、

Kawa: Next, the second half: "They say it's full of cherry-blossom viewers in the spring."

Goto: **Ha⌐ru wa ha⌐nami no hito⌐ de i⌐ppai ni na⌐ru soo desu.**
春は花見の人でいっぱいになるそうです。

Kawa: **Haru wa** means "in spring;" **hanami,** "cherry-blossom viewing;" **hanami no hito** means "cherry-blossom viewers;" **hanami no hito de ippai ni naru,** "become full of cherry-blossom viewers;" **soo desu** here means "it is said that...."

Kawa: Mr. Smith seems interested, and says, "Is that right?"

Goto: **So⌐o desu ka.** そうですか。

Kawa: Mr. Yamamoto suggests, "Shall we take a picture somewhere?"

Goto: **Do⌐ko ka de sha⌐shin o torimasho⌐o.**
どこかで写真をとりましょう。

Kawa: **Doko ka de,** "somewhere;" **shashin,** "photograph;" **Shashin o torimashoo,** "Let's take a picture." Mr. Smith suggests the bridge over there. "What about on that bridge?"

Goto: **A⌐no hashi no ue⌐ wa ⌐do⌐o desu ka.** あの橋の上はどうですか。

Kawa: "Something **no ue**" means "on something;" **ano hashi no ue,** "on that bridge." "What about on that bridge?"

Goto: **A⌐no hashi no ue⌐ wa ⌐do⌐o desu ka.** あの橋の上はどうですか。

Kawa: Mr. Yamamoto agrees. "Good. Let's hurry since it's beginning to get dark."

Goto: **I⌐i desu ne. So⌐rosoro ku⌐raku na⌐tte kimashita kara, i⌐sogimasho⌐o.**
いいですね。そろそろ暗くなってきましたから、いそぎましょう。

Kawa: You remember the third key sentence, don't you, **sorosoro kuraku natte kimashita ne.** Mr. Yamamoto thinks they should hurry up and says, "Let's hurry up."

Goto: **I⌐sogimasho⌐o.** いそぎましょう。

Kawa: You'll now listen to their conversation again.

◆ **Today's Conversation**

Y: **Ka⌐wa no muko⌐o wa A⌐rashiyama to yuu⌐ ya⌐ma⌐ desu.**
川のむこうは嵐山という山です。

S: **Ki⌐ ga ta⌐kusan a⌐tte, ki⌐ree na ya⌐ma⌐ desu ne.**
木がたくさんあって、きれいな山ですね。

Y: **E⌐e, ko⌐no hen wa⌐ sa⌐kura no meesho⌐ de, ha⌐ru wa ha⌐nami no hito⌐ de i⌐ppai ni na⌐ru soo desu.**
ええ、このへんは桜の名所で、春は花見の人でいっぱいになるそうです。

S: **So⌐o desu ka.** そうですか。

Y: **Do⌐ko ka de sha⌐shin o torimasho⌐o.**
どこかで写真をとりましょう。

S: **A⌐no hashi no ue⌐ wa ⌐do⌐o desu ka.** あの橋の上はどうですか。

Y: **I⌐i desu ne. So⌐rosoro ku⌐raku na⌐tte kimashita kara, i⌐sogimasho⌐o.**
いいですね。そろそろ暗くなってきましたから、いそぎましょう。

Kawa: Next, as usual, you'll practice today's vocabulary. Please repeat aloud after Goto-san, who will say each word or phrase twice. First, "tree."

Goto: **Ki⌐.** 木

Kawa: "Cherry-blossom viewers."

Goto: **Ha⌐nami no hito⌐.** 花見の人

Kawa: "Somewhere around here."

Goto: **Ko⌐no hen.** このへん

Kawa: "Many;" "full of."

Goto: **I⌐ppai.** いっぱい

Kawa: Now the key sentences again. This time, just listen to Goto-san. The first key sentence, "There is a mountain across the river."

Goto: **Ka⌐wa no muko⌐o ni ya⌐ma⌐ ga arimasu.**
川のむこうに山があります。

Kawa: Next, the second key sentence, "It's become a little dark."

Goto: **Su⌐ko⌐shi ku⌐raku narima⌐shita.** 少し暗くなりました。

Kawa: The third key sentence, "It's beginning to get dark, isn't it?"

Goto: **So⌐rosoro ku⌐raku na⌐tte ki⌐ma⌐shita ne.**
そろそろ暗くなってきましたね。

Kawa: Now, before we wind up, you'll listen to the whole conversation again.

◆ Today's Conversation

Y: **Ka⌐wa no muko⌐o wa A⌐rashiyama to yuu⌐ ya⌐ma⌐ desu.**
川のむこうは嵐山という山です。

S: **Ki⌐ ga ta⌐kusan a⌐tte, ki⌐ree na ya⌐ma⌐ desu ne.**
木 がたくさんあって、きれいな山ですね。

Y: **E⌐e, ko⌐no hen wa⌐ sa⌐kura no meesho⌐ de, ha⌐ru wa ha⌐nami no hito⌐ de i⌐ppai ni na⌐ru soo desu.**
ええ、このへんは桜の名所で、春は花見の人でいっぱいになるそうです。

S: **So⌐o desu ka.** そうですか。

Y: **Do⌐ko ka de sha⌐shin o torimasho⌐o.**
どこかで写真をとりましょう。

S: Aˈno hashi no ueˈ wa ˈdoˈo desu ka.   あの橋の上はどうですか。

Y: Iˈi desu ne. Soˈrosoro kuˈraku naˈtte kimashita kara, iˈsogimashoˈo.
　　いいですね。そろそろ暗くなってきましたから、いそぎましょう。

Notes

1. Kaˈwa no mukoˈo

Let's review some of relative location words. **Soˈba** ("nearby"); **toˈnari** ("next to"); **naˈka** ("inside"); **maˈe** ("in the front"); **uˈshiro** ("in the back"); **uˈe** ("on top," "up," "above"); **shiˈta** ("under," "down"). All these words are nouns in Japanese. Also note the particle following these words. Depending on the verb that follows, either **ni** or **de** is used. Here are some examples:

  Giˈnkoo wa eˈki no ˈsoˈba ni arimasu. ("The bank is near the station.")
  Kaˈwa no mukoˈo ni yaˈmaˈ ga arimasu. ("Across the river, there is a mountain.")
  Teˈeburu no shitaˈ ni kaˈban ga arimaˈsu. ("Under the table, there is a bag.")
  Kuˈruma no naˈka de ˈmaˈtte imasu kara. ("I'll be waiting for you in the car, so....")
  Kiˈyomizu-dera no soˈba de toˈmodachi ni aimaˈshita. ("I met a friend near Kiyomizu Temple.")

2. Haˈnami no hitoˈ de iˈppai ni naˈru soo desu.

X **de iˈppai** means "something is full of X" or "something is filled with X."

  Koˈno heyaˈ wa ˈhoˈn de iˈppai deˈsu. ("This room is full of books.")
  Niˈchiyoˈobi wa koˈdomo deˈ iˈppai deˈsu. ("It's filled with children on Sundays.")

Iˈppai ni naˈru. ("It becomes full.") The verb **naˈru** means "becomes [something]," or "turns into [something]." With nouns, including the **na**-type nouns, you need the particle **ni**, and with adjectives, the -**ku** form before **naru**.

  Eˈegyoo buˈchoo ni naˈrimaˈshita. ("He became chief of the sales department.")
  Koˈno hen wa zuˈibun benri ni narimashita. ("This area has become quite convenient.")
  Toˈchi ga sukoˈshi ˈyaˈsuku narimashita. ("The land has gotten a little cheaper.")

3. Soˈrosoro kuˈraku naˈtte kimashita kara

Kiˈmaˈshita is appended to the -**te** form of a verb adding the meaning that "the action has been in progress up to now" and suggesting that the action is going to continue. So, **Moˈmiji ga ˈkiˈree ni natte kimashita ne.** means "The foliage has become beautiful." and the implication is that "It will continue to become more beautiful."

  Saˈmuku natte kimashita ne. (saˈmuˈi = "cold")

Additional Vocabulary

uˈmi	（海）	ocean
miˈzuuˈmi	（湖）	lake

ko⌐oen	(公園)	park
ko⌐oban	(交番)	police box
a⌐karui	(明るい)	light (ant. ku⌐rai, dark)

Exercises

1. Substitute the cue words for the underlined parts of the sentence.

    <u>Ka⌐wa</u> no muko⌐o ni <u>ya⌐ma⌐</u> ga arimasu.

    1. ya⌐ma⌐; mi⌐zuu⌐mi
    2. ya⌐ma⌐; u⌐mi
    3. ka⌐wa⌐; o⌐tera
    4. sho⌐kudo⌐osha; byu⌐ffe
    5. ha⌐shi⌐; mi⌐se⌐

2. Answer each question using the phrase given in parentheses.

    Example: Do⌐ko de shashin o torimashoo ka. (ha⌐shi no ue⌐)
              Ha⌐shi no ue⌐ de torimashoo.

    1. Do⌐ko de machimashoo ka. (ha⌐shi no so⌐ba)
    2. Do⌐ko de aimashoo ka. (gi⌐nkoo no ma⌐e)
    3. Do⌐ko de michi o ki⌐kima⌐shita ka. (e⌐ki no mae no ko⌐oban)
    4. Ta⌐naka-san wa do⌐ko ni imasu ka. (ko⌐ojo⌐o no ⌐na⌐ka)
    5. Shi⌐nbun wa do⌐ko ni a⌐rima⌐su ka. (a⌐no teeburu no ue⌐)
    6. Byo⌐oin wa do⌐ko ni arimasu ka. (o⌐oki⌐i michi no mu⌐ko⌐o)
    7. Do⌐ko de yasumimashoo ka. (de⌐pa⌐ato no tonari no ki⌐ssaten)

3. Making necessary changes, substitute the cue word for the word underlined in the sentence.

    Example: Ku⌐rai→Su⌐ko⌐shi <u>ku⌐raku</u> narimashita ne.

    1. a⌐karui
    2. sa⌐mu⌐i
    3. a⌐tataka⌐i
    4. o⌐soi
    5. fu⌐ru⌐i
    6. a⌐kai
    7. shi⌐ro⌐i
    8. chi⌐isa⌐i
    9. a⌐tsu⌐i
    10. ta⌐ka⌐i
    11. be⌐nri
    12. ge⌐nki

13. ki⌉ree
14. fu⌉ben
15. yu⌉umee

4. Respond to each question as in the example, using the verb **na⌉ru** to indicate the change that has taken place.

Example: A: Ko⌈no hen wa <u>be⌉nri desu</u> ka. ("Is this area convenient?")

B: E⌉e, zu⌉ibun ⌈be⌉nri ni narimashita. ("Yes, it's become quite convenient.")

4. 1. A: Kyo⌉o wa <u>sa⌈mu⌉i desu</u> ka.

B: E⌉e, go⌉go kara [   ] naru soo desu yo.

2. A: Ya⌈mamoto-san wa ge⌉nki desu ka.

B: E⌉e, zu⌉ibun [   ] narimashita.

3. A: Ko⌈no ho⌉n wa <u>yu⌈umee de⌉su</u> ka.

B: E⌉e, [   ] na⌉ru to omoimasu yo.

4. A: Mo⌉miji wa ⌈ki⌉ree desu ka.

B: E⌉e, se⌈nshuu yo⌉ri ⌈mo⌉tto [   ] narimashita.

5. A: To⌈chi wa⌉ <u>ta⌈ka⌉i desu</u> ka.

B: E⌉e, ko⌈no hen no tochi wa [   ] natte imasu.

6. A: Fu⌈ru⌉i kuruma wa <u>ya⌈su⌉i desu</u> ka.

B: E⌉e, fu⌈ru⌉i no wa ⌈zu⌉ibun [   ] narimashita ne.

7. A: Ka⌈wa no mukoo no kooen wa <u>ki⌉ree desu</u> ka.

B: E⌉e, ko⌈nogoro wa [   ] narimashita.

8. A: A⌈no tate⌉mono wa <u>fu⌈ru⌉i desu</u> ka.

B: E⌉e, zu⌉ibun [   ] narimashita yo.

9. A: To⌈okyoo wa⌉ ga⌈ikoku⌉jin ga <u>⌈o⌉oi desu</u> ka.

B: E⌉e, ko⌈nogoro wa [   ] narimashita ne.

10. A: Ko⌈ojo⌉o wa <u>o⌈oki⌉i desu</u> ka.

B: E⌉e, i⌈chinen ma⌉e ni [   ] narimashita.

5. **-te kuru.** Following the example, construct sentences.

Example: Ku⌈raku na⌉ru→So⌉rosoro <u>ku⌈raku na⌉tte</u> kimashita ne.

1. sa⌉muku naru
2. te⌉nki ga ⌈wa⌉ruku naru
3. o⌈naka ga suku
4. mi⌈chi ga ko⌉mu
5. hi⌈to ga o⌉oku naru

6. Using the sentences just constructed in Exercise 5 for A, practice the conversation between A and B.

Example: A: So⌐rosoro ku⌐raku na⌐tte kimashita ne.
B: So⌐o desu ne. I⌐so⌐ide ka⌐erimasho⌐o.

7. Using the cue in parentheses, respond to A in Japanese.

Example: A: So⌐rosoro ku⌐raku na⌐tte kimashita ne.
B: (Let's hurry home.)
E⌐e, so⌐o desu ne. I⌐so⌐ide ka⌐erimasho⌐o. (or Ha⌐yaku ka⌐erimasho⌐o.)

1. A: To⌐chi ga zu⌐ibun ⌐ya⌐suku natte kimashita ne.
   B: E⌐e, so⌐o desu ne. (Let's buy a piece of land.)

2. A: Sa⌐too-san no ⌐o⌐kusan wa ⌐do⌐o desu ka.
   B: (She's gotten quite healthy.)

3. A: Ko⌐no hen wa⌐ a⌐tarashi⌐i mise ga ⌐o⌐oku narimashita ne.
   B: E⌐e. (It's gotten convenient.)

4. A: Ko⌐nban wa ⌐sa⌐muku naru deshoo ka.
   B: I⌐ie, (They say it's going to warm up.)

5. A: O⌐soku narim⌐ashita ne.
   B: (Yes, let's go by cab.)

6. A: Do⌐ko ka de ya⌐sumimasho⌐o ka.
   B: (Yes, how about at the coffee shop in front of the bank?)

7. A: Do⌐ko de shashin o torimashoo ka.
   B: (How about on the bridge?)

8. A: Ko⌐no hen wa⌐ sa⌐kura de yuumee de⌐su.
   B: So⌐o desu ka. Ja, ha⌐ru ni wa (it must be filled with people.)

Answers ────────────────────────────────

1. 1. Ya⌐ma no muko⌐o ni mi⌐zuu⌐mi ga arimasu.
   2. Ya⌐ma no muko⌐o ni ⌐u⌐mi ga arimasu.
   3. Ka⌐wa no muko⌐o ni o⌐tera ga arima⌐su.
   4. Sho⌐kudo⌐osha no mu⌐ko⌐o ni ⌐byu⌐ffe ga arimasu.
   5. Ha⌐shi no muko⌐o ni mi⌐se⌐ ga arimasu.

2. 1. Ha⌐shi no so⌐ba de ma⌐chimasho⌐o.
   2. Gi⌐nkoo no ma⌐e de a⌐imasho⌐o.
   3. E⌐ki no mae no ko⌐oban de kikima⌐shita.
   4. Ko⌐ojo⌐o no ⌐na⌐ka ni i⌐ma⌐su.
   5. A⌐no teeburu no ue⌐ ni arimasu.
   6. O⌐oki⌐i michi no mu⌐ko⌐o ni arimasu.
   7. De⌐pa⌐ato no to⌐nari no kissaten de yasumimasho⌐o.

3. 1. Su⌜ko⌝shi a⌜karuku narima⌝shita ne.
    2. Su⌜ko⌝shi ⌜sa⌝muku narimashita ne.
    3. Su⌜ko⌝shi a⌜tata⌝kaku narimashita ne.
    4. Su⌜ko⌝shi o⌜soku narima⌝shita ne.
    5. Su⌜ko⌝shi ⌜fu⌝ruku narimashita ne.
    6. Su⌜ko⌝shi a⌜kaku narima⌝shita ne.
    7. Su⌜ko⌝shi ⌜shi⌝roku narimashita ne.
    8. Su⌜ko⌝shi ⌜chi⌝isaku narimashita ne.
    9. Su⌜ko⌝shi ⌜a⌝tsuku narimashita ne.
    10. Su⌜ko⌝shi ⌜ta⌝kaku narimashita ne.
    11. Su⌜ko⌝shi ⌜be⌝nri ni narimashita ne.
    12. Su⌜ko⌝shi ⌜ge⌝nki ni narimashita ne.
    13. Su⌜ko⌝shi ⌜ki⌝ree ni narimashita ne.
    14. Su⌜ko⌝shi ⌜fu⌝ben ni narimashita ne.
    15. Su⌜ko⌝shi yu⌜umee ni narima⌝shita ne.

4. 1. E⌝e, go⌝go kara ⌜sa⌝muku naru soo desu yo.
    2. E⌝e, zu⌜ibun ⌜ge⌝nki ni narimashita.
    3. E⌝e, yu⌜mee ni na⌝ru to omoimasu yo.
    4. E⌝e, se⌜nshuu yo⌝ri ⌜mo⌝tto kiree ni narimashita.
    5. E⌝e, ko⌜no hen no tochi wa ta⌝kaku natte imasu.
    6. E⌝e, fu⌜ru⌝i no wa ⌜zu⌝ibun ⌜ya⌝suku narimashita ne.
    7. E⌝e, ko⌜nogoro wa ki⌝ree ni narimashita.
    8. E⌝e, zu⌜ibun ⌜fu⌝ruku narimashita yo.
    9. E⌝e, ko⌜nogoro wa o⌝oku narimashita ne.
    10. E⌝e, i⌜chinen ma⌝e ni ⌜o⌝okiku narimashita.

5. 1. So⌝rosoro ⌜sa⌝muku natte kimashita ne.
    2. So⌝rosoro ⌜te⌝nki ga ⌜wa⌝ruku natte kimashita ne.
    3. So⌝rosoro o⌜naka ga suite kima⌝shita ne.
    4. So⌝rosoro mi⌜chi ga ko⌝nde kimashita ne.
    5. So⌝rosoro hi⌜to ga o⌝oku natte kimashita ne.

7. 1. So⌝o desu ne. To⌜chi o kaimasho⌝o.
    2. Zu⌜ibun ⌜ge⌝nki ni natte kimashita. (or na⌜rima⌝shita.)
    3. E⌝e. Be⌝nri ni narimashita.
    4. I⌝ie, a⌜tataka⌝ku naru soo desu yo.
    5. E⌝e, ta⌝kushii de ikimashoo.
    6. So⌝o desu ne. Gi⌜nkoo no ma⌝e no ki⌜ssaten wa do⌝o desu ka.
    7. Ha⌜shi no ue⌝ wa ⌜do⌝o desu ka.
    8. So⌝o desu ka. Ja, ha⌜ru ni wa hi⌜to de⌝ i⌜ppai ni na⌝ru deshoo ne.

LESSON
41

NI⌈JO⌉O-JOO DE
二条城で
At Nijo Castle

	Today's Conversation

Smith: **Ko⌈ko de⌉ ku⌈tsu⌉ o nu⌈ga⌉nakereba na⌈rimase⌉n ka.**

ここでクツを脱がなければなりませんか。

Do we have to take off our shoes here?

Yamamoto: **E⌉e, ku⌈tsu⌉ o ⌈nu⌉ide ⌈na⌉ka o mi⌈masho⌉o.**

ええ、クツを脱いで中を見ましょう。

Yes. Let's take off our shoes and look around inside.

. . . .

Smith: **Hi⌉rokute ri⌈ppa na heya⌉ desu ne. To⌈konoma ni⌉ mo fu⌈suma ni⌉ mo ⌈e⌉ ga ⌈ka⌉ite arimasu ne.**

広くて立派な部屋ですね。床の間にもふすまにも絵がかいてありますね。

This is a spacious and gorgeous room. There are pictures painted in the alcove and on the sliding doors.

Yamamoto: **Ko⌈no shiro wa⌉ Sho⌈ogun ga Kyo⌉oto e ki⌈ta⌉ toki ni tsu⌈katta⌉ n desu.**

この城は将軍が京都へ来たときに使ったんです。

This castle was used by the Shogun when he came to Kyoto.

Smith: **So⌉o desu ka. Sho⌈ogun wa zu⌉ibun ka⌈nemo⌉chi**

datta n desu ne.
そうですか。将軍はずいぶん金持ちだったん
ですね。
Is that so? They were very rich, weren't they?

NIJOO-JOO DE
二条城で
At Nijo Castle

Kawa: Today, in Lesson 41, you'll hear Mr. Smith and Mr. Yamamoto at Nijo Castle in Kyoto. The first key sentence you'll learn today is, "It's a spacious and fine room, isn't it?"

Goto: **Hi]rokute ri[ppa na heya] desu ne.** 広くて立派な部屋ですね。

Kawa: "Spacious" is **hiroi,** and "fine," **rippa na.** When you use words like **hiroi** and **rippa na** together, you shouldn't use **to** for "and," as in **hiroi to rippa na heya.** That's wrong. The correct expression is **hirokute rippa na heya.** Again, "It's a spacious and fine room, isn't it?"

Goto: **Hi]rokute ri[ppa na he[ya] desu ne.** 広くて立派な部屋ですね。

Kawa: Let's have some practice. "It's a spacious and beautiful room, isn't it?" "Beautiful," **kiree na.**

Goto: **Hi]rokute [ki]ree na he[ya] desu ne.** 広くてきれいな部屋ですね。

Kawa: Then, "It's a tall and fine building, isn't it?" "Tall," **takai,** which is changed to **takute.**

Goto: **Ta]kakute ri[ppa na] ta[te]mono desu ne.**
高くて立派な建物ですね。

Kawa: How about a car? **Kuruma.** "It's a large and fine car, isn't it?" "Large," **ookii,** and the same rule applies…**ookikute.**

Goto: **O]okikute ri[ppa na] ku[ruma de]su ne.** 大きくて立派な車ですね。

Kawa: Then, "a room" again. "It's a spacious and quiet room, isn't it?" "Quiet" is **shizuka na.**

Goto: **Hi]rokute [shi]zuka na he[ya] desu ne.** 広くて静かな部屋ですね。

Kawa: Next, the second key sentence. "We must take off our shoes." You see, all visitors are expected to do so in Nijo Castle. "Shoes" is **kutsu;** "take off," **nugu;** "not to take off" is **nuganai,** and "must take off" is **nuganakereba narimasen.** "We must take off our shoes."

Goto: **Ku[tsu] o nu[ga]nakereba na[rimase]n.**
クツを脱がなければなりません。

Kawa: Next, the opposite of "take off," **nugu**, is to "put on," **haku**, which is changed likewise to **hakanakereba narimasen**. "We must put our shoes on."

Goto: **Ku⌈tsu⌉ o ha⌈kana⌉kereba na⌈rimase⌉n.**
クツをはかなければなりません。

Kawa: To say "we put on clothes," we use a different word, **kiru**, not **haku**. "Must put on" is **kinakereba narimasen**. "Coat" is **uwagi**. "We must put our coats on."

Goto: **U⌈wagi o kina⌉kereba na⌈rimase⌉n.**
うわぎを着なければなりません。

Kawa: What about "We must get up early." "Get up," **okiru**. "Not to get up" is **okinai**, and "must get up" is **okinakereba narimasen**. "Early" is **hayaku**. "We must get up early."

Goto: **Ha⌉yaku o⌈ki⌉nakereba na⌈rimase⌉n.** 早く起きなければなりません。

Kawa: So much for "must," **nakereba narimasen**. Our third key sentence is "He was very wealthy, wasn't he?" "He," **ano hito**.

Goto: **A⌈no⌉ hito, ma⌉e wa ka⌈nemo⌉chi datta n desu ne.**
あの人、前は金持ちだったんですね。

Kawa: **Mae wa** means "before;" **kanemochi**, "rich." **Datta** in **datta n desu ne** is the plain form of **deshita**, "was." Adding **n desu ne** to **datta**, **datta n desu ne** expresses a strong or exclamatory feeling about the fact that he was indeed very wealthy before. "He was very wealthy, wasn't he?"

Goto: **A⌈no⌉ hito, ma⌉e wa ka⌈nemo⌉chi datta n desu ne.**
あの人、前は金持ちだったんですね。

Kawa: Shall we then say, "He was very kind, wasn't he?" "Kind," **shinsetsu**.

Goto: **A⌈no⌉ hito, ma⌉e wa ⌈shi⌉nsetsu datta n desu ne.**
あの人、前は親切だったんですね。

Kawa: How about "He was full of spirits, wasn't he?" "Full of spirits," **genki**.

Goto: **A⌈no⌉ hito, ma⌉e wa ⌈ge⌉nki datta n desu ne.**
あの人、前は元気だったんですね。

♪ **Station Break** ‖‖‖

Kawa: In the second half of this program, we'll discuss each dialogue as usual. Listen to the whole conversation first.

◆ **Today's Conversation**

S: **Ko⌈ko de⌉ ku⌈tsu⌉ o nu⌈ga⌉nakereba na⌈rimase⌉n ka.**
ここでクツを脱がなければなりませんか。

Y: E⌐e, ku⌐tsu⌐ o ⌐nu⌐ide ⌐na⌐ka o mi⌐masho⌐o.
えe、クツを脱いで中を見ましょう。

· ·

S: Hi⌐rokute ri⌐ppa na heya⌐ desu ne. To⌐konoma ni⌐ mo fu⌐suma ni⌐ mo ⌐e⌐ ga ⌐ka⌐ite arimasu ne.
広くて立派な部屋ですね。床の間にもふすまにも絵がかいてありますね。

Y: Ko⌐no shiro wa⌐ Sho⌐ogun ga Kyo⌐oto e ki⌐ta⌐ toki ni tsu⌐katta⌐ n desu. この城は将軍が京都へ来たときに使ったんです。

S: So⌐o desu ka. Sho⌐ogun wa zu⌐ibun ka⌐nemo⌐chi datta n desu ne.
そうですか。将軍はずいぶん金持ちだったんですね。

Kawa: Next, you'll listen to its English version.

◆ **Same Conversation in English**

S: Do we have to take off our shoes here?
Y: Yes. Let's take off our shoes and look around inside.

· ·

S: This is a spacious and gorgeous room. There are pictures painted in the alcove and on the sliding doors.
Y: This castle was used by the Shogun when he came to Kyoto.
S: Is that so? They were very rich, weren't they?

Kawa: Now we study each dialogue. At the entrance of the castle, Mr. Smith asks Mr. Yamamoto if he has to take his shoes off. "Do we have to take off our shoes here?"

Goto: Ko⌐ko de⌐ ku⌐tsu⌐ o nu⌐ga⌐nakereba na⌐rimase⌐n ka.
ここでクツを脱がなければなりませんか。

Kawa: You know it's based on the second key sentence. "Yes. Let's take off our shoes and look around inside," says Mr. Yamamoto.

Goto: E⌐e, ku⌐tsu⌐ o ⌐nu⌐ide ⌐na⌐ka o mi⌐masho⌐o.
えe、クツを脱いで中を見ましょう。

Kawa: **Nuide** is the **-te** or **-de** form of **nugu**, "take off," meaning "take off and…." **Naka**, "inside;" **mimashoo**, "let's look around." They are now inside the castle. Mr. Smith exclaims, "This is a spacious and fine room. There are pictures painted both in the alcove and on the sliding doors."

Goto: Hi⌐rokute ri⌐ppa na heya⌐ desu ne. To⌐konoma ni⌐ mo fu⌐suma ni⌐ mo ⌐e⌐ ga ⌐ka⌐ite arimasu ne.
広くて立派な部屋ですね。床の間にもふすまにも絵がかいてありますね。

Kawa: Of course, the first half is the first key sentence. **Tokonoma** is a "traditional alcove," and **fusuma,** "sliding doors." **Ni, in tokonoma ni** and **fusuma ni,** means either "in" or "on." "In the alcove" and "on the sliding doors" **kaite arimasu,** "there's something painted." **E** means "picture." There are pictures painted both in the alcove and on the sliding doors."

Goto: **To⌈konoma ni⌉ mo fu⌈suma ni⌉ mo ⌈e⌉ ga ⌈ka⌉ite arimasu ne.**
床の間にもふすまにも絵がかいてありますね。

Kawa: **Mo** in **ni mo** means "also" or "too." Mr. Yamamoto explains the history of the castle. "The shoguns used this castle when they came to Kyoto."

Goto: **Ko⌈no shiro wa⌉ Sho⌈ogun ga Kyo⌉oto e ki⌈ta⌉ toki ni tsu⌈katta⌉ n desu.** この城は将軍が京都へ来たときに使ったんです。

Kawa: **Kono shiro** means "this castle." The shogun is a tycoon in Japan's feudal times. **Shoogun ga Kyooto e kita,** "the shoguns came to Kyoto;" **toki ni,** "when." So, **Shoogun ga Kyooto e kita toki ni,** "when the shoguns came to Kyoto." **Tsukatta n desu** means "used." Again, "The shoguns used this castle when they came to Kyoto."

Goto: **Ko⌈no shiro wa⌉ Sho⌈ogun ga Kyo⌉oto e ki⌈ta⌉ toki ni tsu⌈katta⌉ n desu.** この城は将軍が京都へ来たときに使ったんです。

Kawa: Mr. Smith seems to be impressed with the financial power of the shoguns. "Is that so. The shoguns were very wealthy, weren't they?" This is our third key sentence, as you remember.

Goto: **So⌉o desu ka. Shoogun wa zuibun kanemochi datta n desu ne.**
そうですか。将軍はずいぶん金持ちだったんですね。

Kawa: Now you'll listen to the whole conversation again.

◆ **Today's Conversation**

S: **Ko⌈ko de⌉ ku⌈tsu⌉ o nu⌈ga⌉nakereba na⌈rimase⌉n ka.**
ここでクツを脱がなければなりませんか。

Y: **E⌉e, ku⌈tsu⌉ o ⌈nu⌉ide ⌈na⌉ka o mi⌈masho⌉o.**
ええ、クツを脱いで中を見ましょう。

· ·

S: **Hi⌉rokute ri⌈ppa na heya⌉ desu ne. To⌈konoma ni⌉ mo fu⌈suma ni⌉ mo ⌈e⌉ ga ⌈ka⌉ite arimasu ne.**
広くて立派な部屋ですね。床の間にもふすまにも絵がかいてありますね。

Y: **Ko⌈no shiro wa⌉ Sho⌈ogun ga Kyo⌉oto e ki⌈ta⌉ toki ni tsu⌈katta⌉ n desu.** この城は将軍が京都へ来たときに使ったんです。

S: **So⌉o desu ka. Sho⌈ogun wa zu⌉ibun ka⌈nemo⌉chi datta n desu ne.**
そうですか。将軍はずいぶん金持ちだったんですね。

Kawa: You'll now review today's vocabulary. Please repeat aloud after Goto-san, who'll say each word or phrase twice. First, "shoes."

Goto: **Ku⌈tsu⌉.** クツ

Kawa: "Picture," "painting."

Goto: **E⌉.** 絵

Kawa: "Castle."

Goto: **Shi⌈ro.** 城

Kawa: "Rich."

Goto: **Ka⌈nemo⌉chi.** 金持ち

Kawa: Now, today's key sentences. This time, just listen to Goto-san. Today's first key sentence is, "This is a spacious and fine room, isn't it?"

Goto: **Hi⌉rokute ri⌈ppa na heya⌉ desu ne.** 広くて立派な部屋ですね。

Kawa: The second key sentence, "We have to take off our shoes."

Goto: **Ku⌈tsu⌉ o nu⌈ga⌉nakereba na⌈rimase⌉n.**
クツを脱がなければなりません。

Kawa: The third key sentence, "He was very wealthy, wasn't he?"

Goto: **A⌈no⌉ hito, ma⌈e wa ka⌈nemo⌉chi datta n desu ne.**
あの人、前は金持ちだったんですね。

Kawa: Now, before we wind up, let's listen to the whole dialogue again.

◆ **Today's Conversation**

S: **Ko⌈ko de⌉ ku⌈tsu⌉ o nu⌈ga⌉nakereba na⌈rimase⌉n ka.**
ここでクツを脱がなければなりませんか。

Y: **E⌉e, ku⌈tsu⌉ o ⌈nu⌉ide ⌈na⌉ka o mi⌈masho⌉o.**
ええ、クツを脱いで中を見ましょう。

. . . .

S: **Hi⌉rokute ri⌈ppa na heya⌉ desu ne. To⌈konoma ni⌉ mo fu⌈suma ni⌉ mo ⌈e⌉ ga ⌈ka⌉ite arimasu ne.**
広くて立派な部屋ですね。床の間にもふすまにも絵がかいてありますね。

Y: **Ko⌈no shiro wa⌉ Sho⌈ogun ga Kyo⌉oto e ki⌈ta⌉ toki ni tsu⌈katta⌉ n desu.**
この城は将軍が京都へ来たときに使ったんです。

S: **So⌉o desu ka. Sho⌈ogun wa zu⌉ibun ka⌈nemo⌉chi datta n desu ne.**
そうですか。将軍はずいぶん金持ちだったんですね。

Notes

1. Ku⌐tsu⌐ o <u>nu⌐ga⌐nakereba</u> <u>narimasen</u>.

-na⌐kereba narimasen (or its informal equivalent, -na⌐kereba na⌐ra⌐nai) expresses "obligation" or "a requirement which needs to be fulfilled." "Have to…" and "Must…" are possible translations. Literally it means "It won't do if you don't…." With verbs, start from the negative form, change the final-i to-kereba and add naranai or narimasen.

("go")   i⌐ku→i⌐kana⌐i→i⌐kana⌐kereba narimasen
("eat")   ta⌐be⌐ru→ta⌐be⌐nai→ta⌐be⌐nakereba narimasen
("do")   su⌐ru→shi⌐nai→shi⌐na⌐kereba narimasen

With nouns (including na-type nouns), add de ⌐na⌐kereba narimasen.

Ni⌐hongo de na⌐kereba narimasen. ("It's got to be in the Japanese language.")
Ki⌐ree de nakereba narimasen. ("It has to be pretty" or "clean.")

2. Hi⌐rokute ri⌐ppa na heya⌐ desu.

In Lesson 22, you learned to use **de** to combine a **na**-type noun with another qualifier, as in **Shi⌐zuka de ⌐i⌐i desu ne.** ("It's quiet and nice.")
To combine an adjective with another qualifying word, you use the -**te** form of the adjective. For example, to combine **O⌐oki⌐i (desu)** with **I⌐i (desu)**, you change **o⌐oki⌐i** to **o⌐okikute; O⌐okikute ⌐i⌐i desu.**

3. Ka⌐nemo⌐chi datta <u>n desu ne</u>.

…**n desu ne** is appended to add the meaning "I just realized that…" or "…<u>is</u> true, isn't it?" or "Now I found out that…."

A: **Shi⌐ta ni⌐ o⌐fu⌐ro ga arimasu ga, i⌐chido⌐ ni ni⌐juunin gu⌐rai hairemasu.**
B: **O⌐oki⌐i n desu ne.**

A: **E⌐ki kara to⌐oi⌐ desu ka.**
B: **I⌐ie, ni⌐fun gu⌐rai desu.**
A: **Zu⌐ibun chi⌐ka⌐i n desu ne.**

A: **A⌐no mise⌐ wa o⌐hi⌐ru wa hi⌐to de⌐ i⌐ppai de⌐su yo.**
B: **Yu⌐umee na⌐ n desu ne.**
A: **E⌐e, ya⌐sukute o⌐ishi⌐i desu kara ne.**

Additional Vocabulary

ku⌐tsu⌐ o haku	（クツをはく）	to put on shoes (**haku** is used for clothing worn on or below the waist, e.g., trousers; socks; shoes; etc.)
u⌐wagi o⌐ ki⌐ru	（うわぎを着る）	to put on a jacket
ne⌐kutai o shi⌐me⌐ru	（ネクタイをしめる）	to put on a necktie
na⌐ka e ⌐ha⌐iru	（中へ入る）	to go inside
so⌐to e ⌐de⌐ru	（外へ出る）	to go outside

Exercises

1. Following the example, use the cues to form sentences.

Example: hi⌐roi; ri⌐ppa; he⌐ya⌐→Hi⌐rokute ri⌐ppa na heya⌐ desu ne.

1. shi⌐ro⌐i; ki⌐ree; ta⌐te⌐mono
2. ta⌐ka⌐i; ri⌐ppa; ta⌐te⌐mono
3. a⌐kai; ki⌐ree; ku⌐ruma
4. o⌐oki⌐i; ri⌐ppa; ku⌐ruma
5. hi⌐ro⌐i; shi⌐zuka; he⌐ya⌐
6. hi⌐ro⌐i; ri⌐ppa; ko⌐ojo⌐o
7. o⌐oki⌐i; ki⌐ree; ko⌐oen

2. First change the verb of the cue to its negative informal form. Then form sentences using the "...have to..." pattern.

Example: Kyo⌐oto e iku→i⌐kana⌐i→Kyo⌐oto e i⌐kana⌐kereba narimasen.

1. Ku⌐tsu⌐ o ⌐nu⌐gu.
2. Ku⌐tsu⌐ o ha⌐ku.
3. A⌐sa ⌐ha⌐yaku o⌐ki⌐ru.
4. Ko⌐nban de⌐kakeru.
5. U⌐wagi o kiru.
6. Ne⌐kutai o shi⌐me⌐ru.
7. I⌐so⌐ide ⌐ka⌐eru.
8. Na⌐ka e ⌐ha⌐iru.
9. So⌐to e ⌐de⌐ru.
10. O⌐kane o hara⌐u.

3. Unite the two cue sentences to form a single sentence using the "Let's... and..." pattern.

Example: Ku⌐tsu⌐ o ⌐nu⌐gu. Na⌐ka e ⌐ha⌐iru.→Ku⌐tsu⌐ o ⌐nu⌐ide, na⌐ka e ha⌐irimasho⌐o.

1. Ha⌐yaku o⌐ki⌐ru. Ha⌐nami⌐ ni dekakeru.
2. U⌐wagi o kiru. Sho⌐kudoo ni iku.
3. Na⌐ka e ⌐ha⌐iru. E⌐ o ⌐mi⌐ru.
4. I⌐so⌐ide ⌐ka⌐eru. Te⌐rebi o ⌐mi⌐ru.
5. A⌐no mise⌐ ni yo⌐ru. O⌐miyage o kau.

4. Following the example, use the cue sentences to form dialogue in which A uses a "Must I...?" question and B answers with "Yes, please...."

Example: Ku⌐tsu⌐ o ⌐nu⌐gu.
A: Ku⌐tsu⌐ o nu⌐ga⌐nakereba narimasen ka.
B: E⌐e, nu⌐ide kudasai.

1. Ne⌐kutai o shi⌐me⌐ru.
2. I⌐so⌐ide ⌐ka⌐eru.
3. A⌐shita⌐ made ni ⌐ke⌐nsa suru.
4. Ki⌐ppu o kau.
5. Pe⌐n o tsukau.
6. Sha⌐shin o to⌐ru.
7. U⌐wagi o kiru.
8. A⌐shita ha⌐yaku kuru.
9. To⌐chi o uru.
10. Chi⌐zu o mo⌐tte ku⌐ru.

5. What do you say in Japanese when you want to:

1. ask if you have to take your jacket off?
2. ask if you need to have a necktie on?
3. tell your friend that you bought it when you went to Shinjuku?
4. tell your friend that you saw Kiyomizu Temple when you went to Kyoto last year?
5. tell your friend that you bought these shoes when you went to Hong Kong?
6. suggest the group go outside?
7. ask your friend to get up early tomorrow?
8. tell your friend that you have to pay the money?
9. tell your friend that you have to buy a souvenir?
10. tell your friend that you have to go home in a hurry?

6. Using words contained in the cue, fill in the blanks in the model sentence.

Model sentence: Ano [   ], mae wa [   ] datta n desu ne.

Example: (kanemochi no hito)→A⌐no⌐ hito, ma⌐e wa ka⌐nemo⌐chi datta n desu ne.

1. shi⌐nsetsu na hito
2. ri⌐ppa na ho⌐teru
3. ki⌐ree na ta⌐te⌐mono
4. ge⌐nki na o⌐toko⌐ no ko
5. ta⌐ihen na shigoto
6. shi⌐zuka na michi

7. Answer the following questions affirmatively. Conclude your answers with **to omoimasu**. Remember before **to omoimasu** you must use the informal form of the verb.

Example: A: Ya⌐mada-san kaerima⌐shita ka.
B: E⌐e, ka⌐etta to omoimasu.

1. A⌈no shiro wa⌉ ri⌈ppa de⌉shita ka.
2. Ko⌈no heya⌉ wa sho⌈ogun ga tsukaima⌉shita ka.
3. A⌈no ooze⌉ no hito wa ha⌈nami no hito de⌉shita ka.
4. Ko⌈no shigoto wa⌉ ta⌈ihen de⌉su ka.
5. Shi⌈ro no na⌉ka wa ⌈ku⌉rakatta desu ka.

Answers

1. 1. Shi⌉rokute ⌈ki⌉ree na ta⌈te⌉mono desu ne.
   2. Ta⌉kakute ri⌈ppa na tate⌉mono desu ne.
   3. A⌈ka⌉kute ⌈ki⌉ree na ku⌈ruma de⌉su ne.
   4. O⌉okikute ri⌈ppa na kuruma de⌉su ne.
   5. Hi⌉rokute ⌈shi⌉zuka na he⌈ya⌉ desu ne.
   6. Hi⌉rokute ri⌈ppa na koojo⌉o desu ne.
   7. O⌉okikute ⌈ki⌉ree na ko⌈oen de⌉su ne.

2. 1. Ku⌈tsu⌉ o nu⌈ga⌉nakereba narimasen.
   2. Ku⌈tsu⌉ o ha⌈kana⌉kereba narimasen.
   3. A⌉sa ⌈ha⌉yaku o⌈ki⌉nakereba narimasen.
   4. Ko⌉nban de⌈kakenakereba narimasen.
   5. U⌈wagi o kina⌉kereba narimasen.
   6. Ne⌉kutai o shi⌈me⌉nakereba narimasen.
   7. I⌈so⌉ide ka⌈era⌉nakereba narimasen.
   8. Na⌉ka e ha⌈ira⌉nakereba narimasen.
   9. So⌉to e de⌉nakereba narimasen.
   10. O⌈kane o harawa⌉nakereba narimasen.

3. 1. Ha⌉yaku okite ha⌈nami⌉ ni de⌈kakemasho⌉o.
   2. U⌈wagi o kite⌉ sho⌈kudoo ni ikimasho⌉o.
   3. Na⌉ka e ⌈ha⌉itte ⌈e⌉ o mi⌈masho⌉o.
   4. I⌈so⌉ide kaette ⌈te⌉rebi o mi⌈masho⌉o.
   5. A⌈no mise⌉ ni yotte o⌈miyage o kaimasho⌉o.

4. 1 A: Ne⌉kutai o shi⌈me⌉nakereba narimasen ka.
      B: E⌉e, ne⌉kutai o ⌈shi⌉mete kudasai.

   2. A: I⌈so⌉ide ka⌈era⌉nakereba narimasen ka.
      B: E⌉e, i⌈so⌉ide ka⌈ette kudasai.

   3. A: A⌈shita⌉ made ni ⌈ke⌉nsa shinakereba narimasen ka.
      B: E⌉e, ke⌉nsa shite kudasai.

   4. A: Ki⌈ppu o kawana⌉kereba narimasen ka.
      B: E⌉e, ka⌈tte kudasa⌉i.

   5. A: Pe⌉n o tsu⌈kawana⌉kereba narimasen ka.
      B: E⌉e, pe⌉n o tsu⌈katte kudasa⌉i.

   6. A: Sha⌈shin o tora⌉nakereba narimasen ka.
      B: E⌉e, to⌉tte kudasai.

   7. A: U⌈wagi o kina⌉kereba narimasen ka.
      B: E⌉e, ki⌈te kudasa⌉i.

   8. A: A⌈shita ha⌉yaku konakereba narimasen ka.
      B: E⌉e, ha⌉yaku ki⌈te⌉ kudasai.

9. A: To⌐chi o urana¬kereba narimasen ka.
    B: E¬e, u⌐tte kudasa¬i.

10. A: Chi¬zu o mo⌐tte ko¬nakereba narimasen ka.
     B: E¬e, mo⌐tte¬ kite kudasai.

5. 1 U⌐wagi o nuga¬nakereba narimasen ka.
    2. Ne¬kutai o shi⌐me¬nakereba narimasen ka.
    3. Shi⌐njuku e itta toki¬ ni kaimashita.
    4. Kyo¬nen ⌐Kyo¬oto e itta toki ni Ki¬yomizu-dera o mima¬shita.
    5. Ho¬nkon e i⌐tta toki¬ ni ko⌐no kutsu¬ o ka⌐ima¬shita.
    6. So¬to e de⌐masho¬o.
    7. A⌐shita ha¬yaku okite kudasai.
    8. O⌐kane o harawa¬nakereba narimasen.
    9. O⌐miyage o kawana¬kereba narimasen.
    10. I⌐so¬ide ka⌐era¬nakereba narimasen.

6. 1 A⌐no¬ hito, ma¬e wa ⌐shi¬nsetsu datta n desu ne.
    2. A⌐no ho¬teru, ma¬e wa ri⌐ppa da¬tta n desu ne.
    3. A⌐no tate¬mono, ma¬e wa ⌐ki¬ree datta n desu ne.
    4. A⌐no otoko¬ no ko, ma¬e wa ⌐ge¬nki datta n desu ne.
    5. A⌐no shigoto, ma¬e wa ta⌐ihen da¬tta n desu ne.
    6. A⌐no michi, ma¬e wa ⌐shi¬zuka datta n desu ne.

7. 1 E¬e, ri⌐ppa da¬tta to omoimasu.
    2. E¬e, sho¬ogun ga tsukatta¬ to omoimasu.
    3. E¬e, ha⌐nami no hito¬ datta to omoimasu.
    4. E¬e, ta⌐ihen da¬ to omoimasu.
    5. E¬e, ⌐ku¬rakatta to omoimasu.

LESSON
42

FU⌐KUSHUU
復習
Review

	Today's Conversation

Ito: Oˈkaerinasaˈi. Kyoˈoto wa ⌐doˈo deshita ka.
お帰りなさい。京都はどうでしたか。
Welcome back. How did you like Kyoto?

Smith: Yoˈkatta desu. Koˈreˈ tsuˈmaraˈnai mono desu ga, oˈmiyage deˈsu.
よかったです。これつまらないものですが、おみやげです。
I enjoyed it very much. Here's a small souvenir for you.

Ito: Maˈa suˈmimaseˈn ne. Naˈn deshoo.
まあ、すみませんね。何でしょう。
That's very nice of you. I wonder what it is.

Smith: Doˈozo aˈkete miˈte kudasai. Seˈnsu deˈsu.
どうぞあけてみて下さい。せんすです。
Please unwrap it and see. It's a fan.

Ito: Kiˈree desu ⌐neˈe.
きれいですねえ。
It's beautiful.

Smith: Kaˈnai ni mo ⌐iˈppon kaimashita.
家内にも一本買いました。
I bought one for my wife, too.

Ito: Doˈomo aˈriˈgatoo gozaimasu.

どうもありがとうございます。
Thank you very much.

. . . .

Ito: **Do⌐nna tokoro e i⌐rasshaima⌐shita ka.**
どんなところへいらっしゃいましたか。
What places did you visit?

Smith: **Ki⌐yomizu-dera ya⌐ Ni⌐jo⌐o-joo o mi⌐ma⌐shita shi, A⌐rashiyama e⌐ mo i⌐ki⌐mashita.**
清水寺や二条城を見ましたし、嵐山へも行きました。
We saw Kiyomizu Temple and Nijo Castle. We went to Arashi-yama, too.

Ito: **So⌐re wa yo⌐katta desu ne. Wa⌐tashi wa⌐ Ki⌐yomizu-dera wa itta koto⌐ ga a⌐rima⌐su kedo, Ni⌐jo⌐o-joo wa ⌐ma⌐da desu.**
それはよかったですね。わたしは清水寺は行ったことがありますけど、二条城はまだです。
That's good. I once went to Kiyomizu Temple, but I haven't been to Nijo Castle.

Smith: **So⌐re kara, Kyo⌐oto no ko⌐toba⌐ mo o⌐moshiro⌐i to o⌐moima⌐shita.**
それから、京都のことばもおもしろいと思いました。
And I was interested in the Kyoto dialect.

Ito: **So⌐o desu ne. To⌐okyoo no kotoba⌐ to ⌐ka⌐nari chi⌐gaima⌐su ne.**
そうですね。東京のことばとかなりちがいますね。
Well, it's considerably different from the language used in Tokyo.

Smith: **Yo⌐ku wa⌐karimase⌐n kedo, To⌐okyoo no kotoba⌐ yori ya⌐waraka⌐i to omoimasu.**
よくわかりませんけど、東京のことばよりやわらかいと思います。
I don't know exactly, but I think it sounds softer than the Tokyo dialect.

Ito: **So⌐o desu ne.**
そうですね。
I agree.

Smith: **O⌐kusan wa ⌐Kyo⌐oto no kotoba ⌐yo⌐ku wa⌐karimas⌐su ka.**

奥さんは京都のことばよくわかりますか。
Do you understand it?

Ito: **Da⌈itai wakarima⌉su. Ji⌈bun de⌉ wa ha⌈nasemase⌉n kedo.**
       だいたいわかります。自分では話せませんけど。
       I can understand most of it, though I can't speak it myself.

FUKUSHUU
復習
Review

Kawa: Today, in Lesson 42, we'll have a review of the previous lessons. As usual, we start with our key sentences. Mr. Smith comes back from Kyoto with a present for Mrs. Ito. He says to Mrs. Ito, "Please unwrap it and see."

Goto: **A⌈kete mi⌉te kudasai.** あけてみて下さい。

Kawa: **Akete** is the **-te** form of **akeru**, "open." **-te mite kudasai** means "do something and see what it's like" or "do something and see what happens." So, here the whole sentence literally means "Please open and see it."

Goto: **A⌈kete mi⌉te kudasai.** あけてみて下さい。

Kawa: Now, let's change a bit. "Please try and read it." The **-te** or **-de** form of **yomu**, "read," is **yonde**.

Goto: **Yo⌉nde mi⌉te kudasai.** 読んでみて下さい。

Kawa: Then, "Please try and eat." Change **taberu** to **tabete**.

Goto: **Ta⌉bete mi⌉te kudasai.** 食べてみて下さい。

Kawa: Our second key sentence is, "I've been to someplace."

Goto: **I⌈tta koto⌉ ga a⌈rima⌉su.** 行ったことがあります。

Kawa: This pattern, **-ta koto ga arimasu**, denotes your experience of having done something. **Itta** is the past form of **iku**, "go." So, "I've been to someplace."

Goto: **I⌈tta koto⌉ ga a⌈rima⌉su.** 行ったことがあります。

Kawa: Next, "I've read it." **Yomu**, "read," is changed to **yonda**, the past form.

Goto: **Yo⌉nda koto⌉ ga a⌈rima⌉su.** 読んだことがあります。

Kawa: How about "I've eaten it."

Goto: **Ta⌉beta koto⌉ ga a⌈rima⌉su.** 食べたことがあります。

Kawa: We've changed **taberu**, "eat," into **tabeta**, the past form. Our third key sentence deals with "I cannot do something," like "I can't speak."

Goto: **Ha⌐nasemase⌐n.** 話せません。

Kawa: "To speak" is **hanashimasu**. "To be able to speak" is **hanasemasu**, and "not to be able to speak" is:

Goto: **Ha⌐nasemase⌐n.** 話せません。

Kawa: Next, "I can't read it." "To read," **yomimasu**. "To be able to read" is **yomemasu**, and "not able to read" is:

Goto: **Yo⌐memase⌐n.** 読めません。

Kawa: Obviously, "I" is omitted. Here's the last one: "You can't go." **Ikimasu**, "to go;" "to be able to go," **ikemasu**, and "not to be able to go:"

Goto: **I⌐kemase⌐n.** 行けません。

Kawa: There, "you" is omitted because it's obvious. Now, in the second half of this session, we'll discuss each dialogue. Listen to their conversation first.

◆ **Today's Conversation**

I: **O⌐kaerinasa⌐i. Kyo⌐oto wa ⌐do⌐o deshita ka.**
お帰りなさい。京都はどうでしたか。

S: **Yo⌐katta desu. Ko⌐re⌐ tsu⌐mara⌐nai mono desu ga, o⌐miyage de⌐su.**
よかったです。これつまらないものですが、おみやげです。

I: **Ma⌐a su⌐mimase⌐n ne. Na⌐n deshoo.**
まあ、すみませんね。何でしょう。

S: **Do⌐ozo a⌐kete mi⌐te kudasai. Se⌐nsu de⌐su.**
どうぞあけてみて下さい。せんすです。

I: **Ki⌐ree desu ⌐ne⌐e.** きれいですねえ。

S: **Ka⌐nai ni mo ⌐i⌐ppon kaimashita.** 家内にも一本買いました。

I: **Do⌐omo a⌐ri⌐gatoo gozaimasu.** どうもありがとうございます。

I: **Do⌐nna tokoro e i⌐rasshaima⌐shita ka.**
どんなところへいらっしゃいましたか。

S: **Ki⌐yomizu-dera ya⌐ Ni⌐jo⌐o-joo o mi⌐ma⌐shita shi, A⌐rashiyama e⌐ mo i⌐ki⌐mashita.**
清水寺や二条城を見ましたし、嵐山へも行きました。

I: **So⌐re wa yo⌐katta desu ne. Wa⌐tashi wa⌐ Ki⌐yomizu-dera wa itta koto⌐ ga a⌐rima⌐su kedo, Ni⌐jo⌐o-joo wa ⌐ma⌐da desu.**
それはよかったですね。わたしは清水寺は行ったことがありますけど、二条城はまだです。

S: So⌈re kara, Kyo⌉oto no ko⌈toba⌉ mo o⌈moshiro⌉i to o⌈moima⌉shita.
　それから、京都のことばもおもしろいと思いました。

I: So⌉o desu ne. To⌈okyoo no kotoba⌉ to ⌈ka⌉nari chi⌈gaima⌉su ne.
　そうですね。東京のことばとかなりちがいますね。

S: Yo⌉ku wa⌈karimase⌉n kedo, To⌈okyoo no kotoba⌉ yori ya⌈waraka⌉i to omoimasu.
　よくわかりませんけど、東京のことばよりやわらかいと思います。

I: So⌉o desu ne.　そうですね。

S: O⌉kusan wa ⌈Kyo⌉oto no kotoba ⌈yo⌉ku wa⌈karimas⌉su ka.
　奥さんは京都のことばよくわかりますか。

I: Da⌈itai wakarima⌉su. Ji⌈bun de⌉ wa ha⌈nasemase⌉n kedo.
　だいたいわかります。自分では話せませんけど。

Kawa: Next, you'll listen to its English version.

◆ **Same Conversation in English**

I: Welcome back. How did you like Kyoto?

S: I enjoyed it very much. Here's a small souvenir for you.

I: That's very nice of you. I wonder what it is.

S: Please unwrap it and see. It's a fan.

I: It's beautiful.

S: I bought one for my wife, too.

I: Thank you very much.

· ·

I: What places did you visit?

S: We saw Kiyomizu Temple and Nijo Castle. We went to Arashi-yama, too.

I: That's good. I once went to Kiyomizu Temple, but I haven't been to Nijo Castle.

S: And I was interested in the Kyoto dialect.

I: Well, it's considerably different from the language used in Tokyo.

S: I don't know exactly, but I think it sounds softer than the Tokyo dialect.

I: I agree.

S: Do you understand it?

I: I can understand most of it, though I can't speak it myself.

Kawa: Now each dialogue. We start with an idiomatic expression for "Welcome back," **okaeri-nasai**, and "How was Kyoto?"

Goto: O⌈kaerinasa⌉i. Kyo⌉oto wa ⌈do⌉o deshita ka.
お帰りなさい。京都はどうでしたか。

Kawa: The tour of Kyoto was wonderful for Mr. Smith. "It was great," he says. "Here's a small souvenir for you."

Goto: Yo⌉⌈re⌉ tsu⌈mara⌉nai mono desu ga, o⌈miyage de⌉su.
よかったです。これつまらないものですが、おみやげです。

Kawa: **Tsumaranai mono** means "a humble present," literally. This is just an idiomatic expression used when giving someone a gift. Mrs. Ito is delighted and says, "That's very nice of you. I wonder what it is."

Goto: Ma⌉a su⌈mimase⌉n ne. Na⌉n deshoo.
まあ、すみませんね。何でしょう。

Kawa: Pay attention to her **sumimasen ne** or **suimasen ne**. She means "Thank you," not "I'm sorry." When given a present, most Japanese refrain from opening it on the spot. Mr. Smith urges her to open it. "Please unwrap it and see. It's a fan."

Goto: Do⌉ozo a⌈kete mi⌉te kudasai. Se⌈nsu de⌉su.
どうぞあけてみて下さい。せんすです。

Kawa: You've recognized the first key sentence, **Akete mite kudasai.** Mrs. Ito does so and admires what she's found in it. "It's beautiful."

Goto: Ki⌉ree desu ⌈ne⌉e.　きれいですねえ。

Kawa: It's a beautiful fan. He also bought one for his wife.

Goto: Ka⌉nai ni mo ⌈i⌉ppon kaimashita.　家内にも一本買いました。

Kawa: You may have noticed **ippon**, which means "one." We count longish objects such as bottles, pencils, and so on in terms of so many **hon**, **bon**, or, **pon**, like two beer bottles, **nihon**, three pencils, **sanbon**, four sticks, **yonhon**, and so on. Mrs. Ito thanks him for the present: "Thank you very much."

Goto: Do⌉omo a⌈ri⌉gatoo gozaimasu.　どうもありがとうございます。

Kawa: Mrs. Ito asks him, "What places did you visit?"

Goto: Do⌉nna tokoro e i⌈rasshaima⌉shita ka.
どんなところへいらっしゃいましたか。

Kawa: He visited various places. "We saw Kiyomizu Temple and Nijo Castle, and…"

Goto: Ki⌈yomizu-dera ya⌉ Ni⌈jo⌉o-joo o mi⌈ma⌉shita shi,
清水寺や二条城を見ましたし、

Kawa: "We went to Arashiyama, too."

Goto: A⌈rashiyama e⌉ mo i⌈ki⌉mashita.　嵐山へも行きました。

Kawa: "That's good," she says.

Goto: So⌈re wa yo⌉katta desu ne.　それはよかったですね。

Kawa: "I once went to Kiyomizu Temple, but…."

Goto: Wa⌈tashi wa⌉ Ki⌈yomizu-dera wa itta koto⌉ ga a⌈rima⌉su kedo.
わたしは清水寺は行ったことがありますけど。

Kawa: Her remark contains the second key sentence, **Itta koto ga arimasu.** She further continues: "…but I haven't been to Nijo Castle yet."

Goto: Ni⌈jo⌉o-joo wa ⌈ma⌉da desu. 二条城はまだです。

Kawa: Mr. Smith found the Kyoto dialect a little different. He says, "And I thought the Kyoto dialect was interesting."

Goto: So⌈re kara, Kyo⌉oto no ko⌈toba⌉ mo o⌈moshiro⌉i to o⌈moima⌉shita.
それから、京都のことばもおもしろいと思いました。

Kawa: Mrs. Ito agrees. "Well, it's considerably different from the language used in Tokyo."

Goto: So⌉o desu ne. To⌈kyoo no kotoba⌉ to ⌈ka⌉nari chi⌈gaima⌉su ne.
そうですね。東京のことばとかなりちがいますね。

Kawa: **Kanari chigaimasu,** "is considerably different." Mr. Smith is modest about his perception of the language. He says, "I don't know exactly, but…."

Goto: Yo⌉ku wa⌈karimase⌉n kedo. よくわかりませんけど。

Kawa: "I think it sounds softer than the Tokyo dialect."

Goto: To⌈kyoo no kotoba⌉ yori ya⌈waraka⌉i to omoimasu.
東京のことばよりやわらかいと思います。

Kawa: "That's true," she agrees.

Goto: So⌉o desu ne. そうですね。

Kawa: Mr. Smith is curious to know… "Do you understand Kyoto dialect?"

Goto: O⌉kusan wa ⌈Kyo⌉oto no kotoba ⌈yo⌉ku wa⌈karimas⌉su ka.
奥さんは京都のことばよくわかりますか。

Kawa: Mrs. Ito's answer: "I can understand most of it, though I can't speak it myself."

Goto: Da⌈itai wakarima⌉su. Ji⌈bun de⌉ wa ha⌈nasemase⌉n kedo.
だいたいわかります。自分では話せませんけど。

Kawa: She said, "…though I can't speak it myself," **jibun de wa hanasemasen kedo** that contains the third key sentence, **hanasemasen.** Now let's review the key sentences again. Just listen to Goto-san. The first key sentence: "Please unwrap it and see."

Goto: A⌈kete mi⌉te kudasai. あけてみて下さい。

Kawa: Next, the second key sentence: "I once went there" or "I've been there once."

Goto: I⌈tta koto⌉ ga a⌈rima⌉su. 行ったことがあります。

Kawa: And the third key sentence: "I can't speak it."

Goto: Ha⌈nasemase⌉n. 話せません。

Kawa: Now, you'll listen to their conversation again.

◆ Today's Conversation

I: O⌐kaerinasa⌐i. Kyo⌐oto wa ⌐do⌐o deshita ka.
お帰りなさい。京都はどうでしたか。

S: Yo⌐katta desu. Ko⌐re⌐ tsu⌐mara⌐nai mono desu ga, o⌐miyage de⌐su.
よかったです。これつまらないものですが、おみやげです。

I: Ma⌐a su⌐mimase⌐n ne. Na⌐n deshoo.
まあ、すみませんね。何でしょう。

S: Do⌐ozo a⌐kete mi⌐te kudasai. Se⌐nsu de⌐su.
どうぞあけてみて下さい。せんすです。

I: Ki⌐ree desu ⌐ne⌐e.　きれいですねえ。

S: Ka⌐nai ni mo ⌐i⌐ppon kaimashita.　家内にも一本買いました。

I: Do⌐omo a⌐ri⌐gatoo gozaimasu.　どうもありがとうございます。

・・・

I: Do⌐nna tokoro e i⌐rasshaima⌐shita ka.
どんなところへいらっしゃいましたか。

S: Ki⌐yomizu-dera ya⌐ Ni⌐jo⌐o-joo o mi⌐ma⌐shita shi, A⌐rashiyama e⌐ mo i⌐ki⌐mashita.
清水寺や二条城を見ましたし、嵐山へも行きました。

I: So⌐re wa yo⌐katta desu ne. Wa⌐tashi wa⌐ Ki⌐yomizu-dera wa itta koto⌐ ga a⌐rima⌐su kedo, Ni⌐jo⌐o-joo wa ⌐ma⌐da desu.
それはよかったですね。わたしは清水寺は行ったことがありますけど、二条城はまだです。

S: So⌐re kara, Kyo⌐oto no ko⌐toba⌐ mo o⌐moshiro⌐i to o⌐moima⌐shita.
それから、京都のことばもおもしろいと思いました。

I: So⌐o desu ne. To⌐okyoo no kotoba⌐ to ⌐ka⌐nari chi⌐gaima⌐su ne.
そうですね。東京のことばとかなりちがいますね。

S: Yo⌐ku wa⌐karimase⌐n kedo, To⌐okyoo no kotoba⌐ yori ya⌐waraka⌐i to omoimasu.
よくわかりませんけど、東京のことばよりやわらかいと思います。

I: So⌐o desu ne.　そうですね。

S: O⌐kusan wa ⌐Kyo⌐oto no kotoba ⌐yo⌐ku wa⌐karimas⌐su ka.
奥さんは京都のことばよくわかりますか。

I: Da⌐itai wakarima⌐su. Ji⌐bun de⌐ wa ha⌐nasemase⌐n kedo.
だいたいわかります。自分では話せませんけど。

Notes

1. -ho⌐n (or **-bo⌐n**, or **-po⌐n**, depending on the preceding sound) is the counter word for long or cylindrical objects.

1	i⌐ppon
2	ni⌐hon
3	sa⌐nbon
4	yo⌐nhon (never **shihon**)
5	go⌐hon
6	ro⌐ppon
7	na⌐na⌐hon (rarely **shi⌐chi⌐hon**)
8	ha⌐ppon or ha⌐chi⌐hon
9	kyu⌐uhon (never **kuhon**)
10	ju⌐ppon
11	ju⌐ui⌐ppon
100	hya⌐ppon
1,000	(i⌐s) **senbon**
10,000	i⌐chimanbon

Like other counters or numbers, these too are used adverbially: **Pe⌐n ga go⌐hon arimasu.** ("There are five pens.") **Bi⌐iru o ⌐nihon nomimashita.** ("I drank two bottles of beer.")

2. X to chi⌐gau. ("It is different from X.")

Particle **to** is used to indicate the thing with which another thing is being compared.
A wa B to o⌐naji de⌐su. ("A is the same as B.") **O⌐naji** ("the same") modifies a noun directly, as in **o⌐naji hito,** "the same person." **Ta⌐naka-san no⌐ to o⌐naji kuruma o kaima⌐shita.** "I bought a car like Mr. Tanaka's."

Additional Vocabulary

Here are some more greetings that are used every day.

I⌐tte mairimasu (or, more informally, **I⌐tte kimasu**) is used when you go out of your home or office.
I⌐tte (i)rasshai (ma⌐se) is used by those who see you off at home or office.
Ta⌐daima is used when you get back home or return to your office.
O⌐kaerinasai(ma⌐se) is used by those who meet you at home or office.

Exercises

1. Substitute the cue for the underlined phrase in the example.

   Example: **O⌐osaka e itta toki, Ya⌐mada-san ni aima⌐shita.**

   1. **Ko⌐ojo⌐o o ke⌐ngaku shima⌐shita.**
   2. **O⌐miyage o kaima⌐shita.**
   3. **O⌐osaka no kotoba⌐ de ha⌐na⌐shite mimashita.**

4. Shi⌐nka⌐nsen ni no⌐rima⌐shita.
5. Fu⌐ji-san ga ⌐yo⌐ku mi⌐ema⌐shita.

2. Combine the two sentences using **toki** ("when").

Example: O⌐osaka e ikima⌐shita. Ya⌐mada-san ni aima⌐shita.
O⌐osaka e itta toki⌐, Ya⌐mada-san ni aima⌐shita.

1. Ko⌐ojoo e ikima⌐shita. A⌐tarashi⌐i seehin o mi⌐ma⌐shita.
2. O⌐tera no na⌐ka ni ha⌐irima⌐shita. Ku⌐tsu⌐ o nu⌐gima⌐shita.
3. Kyo⌐oto ni tsu⌐kima⌐shita. Sa⌐nji-⌐ni⌐juu-⌐ha⌐ppun deshita.
4. Ha⌐nami⌐ ni ikimashita. Sha⌐shin o⌐ ta⌐kusan torima⌐shita.
5. Ku⌐raku na⌐tte kimashita. Su⌐misu-san ga kimashita.
6. Su⌐misu-san ga kimashita. Bi⌐iru o ⌐sa⌐nbon no⌐mima⌐shita.
7. Shi⌐njuku e ikima⌐shita. Ko⌐domo ni omiyage o kaima⌐shita.

3. Say in Japanese.

1. What do you say to the person who just returned from a short trip?
2. Someone welcomed you back by saying, **okaerinasai**. What do you say to him?
3. What do you say when you give a present to someone?
4. How do you ask someone if he has ever been to Kyoto?
5. When you want to say you cannot read **hiragana** yet?
6. Tell your friend that this temple is considerably different from Kiyomizu Temple.
7. Tell your friend that you think the Kyoto dialect is softer than the Tokyo dialect.
8. Tell our friend that you made the box lunch yourself.
9. You are leaving for a short business trip. Your office people said, **Itte rasshaimase**. What do you say to them?
10. You want your friend to try the new coffee. Ask him to drink it and see if he likes it.

4. Read **Today's Conversation** and answer the following questions.

1. Su⌐misu-san wa ⌐do⌐ko kara ka⌐erima⌐shita ka.
2. I⌐too-san no o⌐kusan ni o⌐miyage o kaima⌐shita ka.
3. Na⌐ni o kaimashita ka.
4. I⌐tsu kaimashita ka.
5. Ji⌐bun no o⌐kusan ni mo ka⌐ima⌐shita ka.
6. Su⌐misu-san wa ⌐Kyo⌐oto de ⌐do⌐nna tokoro o mi⌐mashita ka.
7. I⌐too-san no o⌐kusan wa Ki⌐yomizu-dera e itta koto⌐ ga a⌐rima⌐su ka.
8. I⌐too-san no o⌐kusan wa Ni⌐jo⌐o-joo e i⌐tta koto⌐ ga a⌐rima⌐su ka.

9. Su⌐misu-san wa ⌐Kyo⌐oto no ko⌐toba⌐ wa To⌐okyoo no kotoba⌐ to ⌐do⌐o chigau to i⌐ima⌐shita ka.

10. I⌐too-san no o⌐kusan wa ⌐Kyo⌐oto no ko⌐toba⌐ ga ha⌐nasema⌐su ka.

5. You are asked the following questions. Answer in Japanese.

1. Kyo⌐oto e i⌐tta koto⌐ ga a⌐rima⌐su ka.
2. Me⌐esho⌐ e i⌐tta toki, o⌐miyage o kaima⌐shita ka.
3. Do⌐nna o⌐miyage o kaima⌐shita ka.
4. Ni⌐hon no sensu o mi⌐ta koto ga a⌐rima⌐su ka.
5. Kyo⌐oto no ko⌐toba⌐ o ki⌐ita koto⌐ ga a⌐rima⌐su ka.
6. Kyo⌐oto no ko⌐toba⌐ ga ha⌐nasema⌐su ka.
7. (In your country) O⌐toko no hito no kotoba⌐ wa o⌐nna no hito no kotoba⌐ to chi⌐gaima⌐su ka.

Answers

2. 1. Ko⌐ojo⌐o e itta toki, a⌐tarashi⌐i seehin o mi⌐ma⌐shita.
   2. O⌐tera no naka⌐ ni haitta toki, ku⌐tsu⌐ o nugimashita. (Here you can say, O⌐tera no naka⌐ ni hairu toki, ku⌐tsu⌐ o nugimashita. This is because the action of entering the temple had not yet been completed at the time you took off your shoes.)
   3. Kyo⌐oto ni tsuita toki, ⌐sa⌐nji-⌐ni⌐juu-⌐ha⌐ppun deshita.
   4. Ha⌐nami⌐ ni itta toki, sha⌐shin o⌐ ta⌐kusan torima⌐shita.
   5. Ku⌐raku na⌐tte kita toki, ⌐Su⌐misu-san ga kimashita.
   6. Su⌐misu-san ga kita toki, ⌐bi⌐iru o ⌐sa⌐nbon nomimashita.
   7. Shi⌐njuku e itta toki⌐, ko⌐domo ni⌐ o⌐miyage o kaima⌐shita.

3. 1. O⌐kaerinasai.
   2. Ta⌐daima.
   3. Ko⌐re, tsu⌐mara⌐nai mono desu ga, do⌐ozo.
   4. Kyo⌐oto e i⌐tta koto⌐ ga arimasu ka. (If you want to be very polite, Kyo⌐oto e i⌐rassha⌐tta koto ga o⌐ari de⌐su ka.)
   5. Hi⌐ragana wa ma⌐da yo⌐memase⌐n.
   6. Ko⌐no otera wa⌐ Ki⌐yomizu-dera to ka⌐nari chi⌐gaima⌐su ne.
   7. Kyo⌐oto no kotoba wa To⌐okyoo no kotoba⌐ yori ya⌐waraka⌐i to omoimasu.
   8. O⌐bentoo o⌐ ji⌐bun de tsukurima⌐shita.
   9. I⌐tte mairima⌐su.
   10. Ko⌐no koohi⌐i, no⌐nde mite kudasai.

4. 1. Kyo⌐oto kara ka⌐erima⌐shita.
   2. Ha⌐i, ka⌐ima⌐shita.
   3. Se⌐nsu o (i⌐ppon) ka⌐ima⌐shita.
   4. Kyo⌐oto e itta toki, ka⌐ima⌐shita.
   5. Ha⌐i, ka⌐ima⌐shita. O⌐kusan ni mo se⌐nsu o kaima⌐shita.
   6. Ki⌐yomizu-dera ya⌐ Ni⌐jo⌐o-joo o mimashita. A⌐rashiyama e⌐ mo ikimashita.
   7. E⌐e, i⌐tta koto⌐ ga arimasu.
   8. I⌐ie, ma⌐da i⌐tta koto⌐ ga a⌐rimase⌐n. (Or I⌐ie, ma⌐da desu.)
   9. Kyo⌐oto no kotoba no hoo ga ya⌐waraka⌐i to omou to i⌐ima⌐shita.
   10. I⌐ie, ji⌐bun de⌐ wa ha⌐nasemase⌐n.

5. 1. E⌐e, i⌐tta koto⌐ ga arimasu. (Or, I⌐ie, i⌐tta koto⌐ ga a⌐rimase⌐n.)
   2. Ha⌐i, ka⌐ima⌐shita. (Or, I⌐ie, ka⌐imase⌐n deshita.)
   3. [   ] o ka⌐ima⌐shita.
   4. Ha⌐i, mi⌐ta koto ga arimasu. (Or, I⌐ie, a⌐rimasen.)
   5. Ha⌐i, a⌐rima⌐su. (Or, I⌐ie, a⌐rimasen.)
   6. Ha⌐i, ha⌐nasema⌐su. (Or, I⌐ie, ha⌐nasemase⌐n.)
   7. Ha⌐i (su⌐koshi; ka⌐nari; zu⌐ibun) chi⌐gaima⌐su. (Or, I⌐ie, o⌐naji de⌐su.)

LESSON 43

TE˥REBI NO
SU˥POOTSU BA˥NGUMI O MI˥NA˥GARA
テレビのスポーツ番組を見ながら
Watching a Sports Program on TV

	Today's Conversation

Ito: Su˥misu-san no o˥kuni de˥ mo su˥po˥otsu sa˥kan de˥su ka.
スミスさんのおくにでもスポーツ盛んですか。
Is sport popular in your country, too?

Smith: E˥e, fu˥ttobo˥oru ya ˥te˥nisu nado i˥roiro arima˥su. Jo˥gingu o suru hito˥ mo ta˥kusan ima˥su. Ni˥ho˥n to ni˥te ima˥su yo.
ええ、フットボールやテニスなどいろいろあります。ジョギングをする人もたくさんいます。日本と似ていますよ。
Yes. We play football, tennis and various other sports. Many people enjoy jogging, like the Japanese.

Ito: A, ju˥udoo no shi˥ai de˥su yo.
あ、柔道の試合ですよ。
Look! It's a judo match.

Smith: O˥nna no hito˥ desu ne.
女の人ですね。
I see there are women playing.

Ito: Mu˥kashi wa˥ o˥toko no hito ba˥kari deshita ga, ko˥nogoro wa˥ o˥nna no hito˥ mo ya˥ru yo˥o ni na˥rima˥shita.
昔は男の人ばかりでしたが、このごろは女の人もやるようになりました。

> In the past, only men used to play it, but nowadays women do, too.

TEREBI NO SUPOOTSU BANGUMI O MINAGARA
テレビのスポーツ番組を見ながら
Watching a Sports Program on TV

Kawa: Today, in Lesson 43, Mr. Smith watches a sports program on TV at the Itos'. Mrs. Ito asks him, "Is sport popular in your country, too, Mr. Smith?" That's our first key sentence.

Goto: **Su⌐misu-san no o⌐kuni de⌐ mo su⌐po⌐otsu ga sa⌐kan de⌐su ka.**
スミスさんのおくにでもスポーツが盛んですか。

Kawa: **Okuni** in **Sumisu-san no okuni de mo**, "also in your country, Mr. Smith," means "your country," politely mentioned. **De mo** at the end of the same phrase is similar to "also" or "too." **Sakan** means "popular."

Goto: **Su⌐misu-san no o⌐kuni de⌐ mo su⌐po⌐otsu ga sa⌐kan de⌐su ka.**
スミスさんのおくにでもスポーツが盛んですか。

Kawa: Now, substitutions. "Is tennis popular in your country, too, Mr. Smith?" **Te-ni-su** is "tennis" in Japanese.

Goto: **Su⌐misu-san no o⌐kuni de⌐ mo ⌐te⌐nisu ga sa⌐kan de⌐su ka.**
スミスさんのおくにでもテニスが盛んですか。

Kawa: How about "jogging?" "Is jogging popular in your country, too, Mr. Smith?" "Jogging" is **jo-gi-n-gu.**

Goto: **Su⌐misu-san no o⌐kuni de⌐ mo jo⌐gingu ga⌐ sa⌐kan de⌐su ka.**
スミスさんのおくにでもジョギングが盛んですか。

Kawa: Our second key sentence deals with **nado**, which means "and so on," "and so forth," "and many others," like **tenisu ya jogingu nado**, "tennis, jogging and various other sports." Let's try "They sell magazines, books and so on."

Goto: **Za⌐sshi ya ho⌐n nado o u⌐rima⌐su.** 雑誌や本などを売ります。

Kawa: **Zasshi** means "magazine;" **hon,** "book;" **urimasu,** "to sell."

Goto: **Za⌐sshi ya ho⌐n nado o u⌐rima⌐su.** 雑誌や本などを売ります。

Kawa: Next, we buy newspapers and books. "To buy," **kaimasu**; "newspaper," **shinbun**. "We buy newspapers, books and so forth."

Goto: **Shi⌐nbun ya ho⌐n nado o ka⌐ima⌐su.** 新聞や本などを買います。

Kawa: Our third key sentence contains **bakari**, meaning "only." For example, "In the old days, only men used to do judo." "In the old days,"

mukashi wa; "only men," **otoko no hito bakari**; "used to do judo,"
juudo o yarimashita. So, we would say…

Goto:　**Mu⌐kashi wa⌐ o⌐toko no hito ba⌐kari ga ⌐ju⌐udoo o ya⌐rima⌐shita.**
　　　昔は男の人ばかりが柔道をやりました。

Kawa:　But we may contextually omit **juudo o yarimashita**, like our third
　　　key sentence.

Goto:　**Mu⌐kashi wa⌐ o⌐toko no hito ba⌐kari deshita.**
　　　昔は男の人ばかりでした。

Kawa:　And this does mean that it used to be only men who did judo in the
　　　old days. Listen to Goto-san again.

Goto:　**Mu⌐kashi wa⌐ o⌐toko no hito ba⌐kari deshita.**
　　　昔は男の人ばかりでした。

Kawa:　Let's replace men with women, for instance, in the sense that "in
　　　the old days, only women made up their minds to be hairdressers."
　　　As before, "made up their minds to be hairdressers" will be omitted,
　　　so:

Goto:　**Mu⌐kashi wa⌐ o⌐nna no hito ba⌐kari deshita.**
　　　昔は女の人ばかりでした。

Kawa:　How about foreigners and whisky that used to be enjoyed among
　　　people from abroad. "In the old days, only foreigners used to have
　　　whisky," ommitting the reference to whisky. "Foreigners" is
　　　gaikokujin.

Goto:　**Mu⌐kashi wa⌐ ga⌐ikoku⌐jin ⌐ba⌐kari deshita.**
　　　昔は外国人ばかりでした。

Kawa:　Things have changed. Women are engaged in various activities,
　　　which they didn't in the old days. Our fourth key sentence is,
　　　"Nowadays, women have started doing it, too."

Goto:　**Ko⌐nogoro wa⌐ o⌐nna no hito⌐ mo ya⌐ru yo⌐o ni na⌐rima⌐shita.**
　　　このごろは女の人もやるようになりました。

Kawa:　**Konogoro**, "nowadays;" **yaru yoo ni narimashita**, "have started
　　　doing something," "have come to do something." **Yaru** means "do
　　　something."

Goto:　**Ko⌐nogoro wa⌐ o⌐nna no hito⌐ mo ya⌐ru yo⌐o ni na⌐rima⌐shita.**
　　　このごろは女の人もやるようになりました。

Kawa:　Now substitutions. "Nowadays, women have started going to
　　　university." "Women," **onna no hito**; "have started going," **iku yoo
　　　ni narimashita**; "to university," **daigaku e**.

Goto:　**Ko⌐nogoro wa⌐ o⌐nna no hito⌐ mo dai⌐gaku e iku yo⌐o ni na⌐ri-
　　　ma⌐shita.**
　　　このごろは女の人も大学へ行くようになりました。

Kawa:　Some kinds of work used to be done only by men. But it's different these days. Nowadays, women have started doing this work. "Do this work," **kono shigoto o suru**.

Goto: **Ko⌐nogoro wa⌐ o⌐nna no hito⌐ mo ko⌐no shigoto o suru yo⌐o ni na⌐ri-ma⌐shita.**
このごろは女の人もこの仕事をするようになりました。

♪ **Station Break** 〰〰〰〰〰〰〰〰〰〰〰〰〰〰〰〰〰〰〰〰〰〰〰〰〰〰〰〰〰

Kawa: In the second half of this program, we'll discuss each dialogue as usual. Listen to the whole conversation first.

◆ **Today's Conversation**

I: **Su⌐misu-san no o⌐kuni de⌐ mo su⌐po⌐otsu sa⌐kan de⌐su ka.**
スミスさんのおくにでもスポーツさかんですか。

S: **E⌐e, fu⌐ttobo⌐oru ya ⌐te⌐nisu nado i⌐roiro arima⌐su. Jo⌐gingu o suru hito⌐ mo ta⌐kusan ima⌐su. Ni⌐ho⌐n to ni⌐te ima⌐su yo.**
ええ、フットボールやテニスなどいろいろあります。ジョギングをする人もたくさんいます。日本と似ていますよ。

I: **A, ju⌐udoo no shi⌐ai de⌐su yo.** あ、柔道の試合ですよ。

S: **O⌐nna no hito⌐ desu ne.** 女の人ですね。

I: **Mu⌐kashi wa⌐ o⌐toko no hito ba⌐kari deshita ga, ko⌐nogoro wa⌐ o⌐nna no hito⌐ mo ya⌐ru yo⌐o ni na⌐rima⌐shita.**
昔は男の人ばかりでしたが、このごろは女の人もやるようになりました。

Kawa: Next, you'll listen to its English version.

◆ **Same Conversation in English**

I: Is sport popular in your country, too?

S: Yes. We play football, tennis and various other sports. Many people enjoy jogging, like the Japanese.

I: Look! It's a judo match.

S: I see there are women playing.

I: In the past, only men used to play it, but nowadays women do, too.

Kawa: Now we study each dialogue. Mrs. Ito would like to know about sports in Mr. Smith's country. She asks him, "Is sport popular in your country, too, Mr. Smith?"

Goto: **Su⌐misu-san no o⌐kuni de⌐ mo su⌐po⌐otsu sa⌐kan de⌐su ka.**
スミスさんのおくにでもスポーツ盛んですか。

Kawa: This is today's first key sentence. Mr. Smith says, "Yes. We play football, tennis and various other sports...." "Football" is **futtobooru**; "all kinds," **iroiro**.

Goto: **E⌐e, fu⌐ttobo⌐oru ya ⌐te⌐nisu nado i⌐roiro arima⌐su.**
えぇ、フットボールやテニスなどいろいろあります。

Kawa: He also refers to many people who enjoy jogging. "There are a lot of people who go jogging, too." "There are a lot of," **takusan arimasu**. "People who go jogging," **jogingu o suru hito**.

Goto: **Jo⌐gingu o suru hito⌐ mo ta⌐kusan ima⌐su.**
ジョギングをする人もたくさんいます。

Kawa: **Mo** after **hito** ("people") in **hito mo** means "also" or "too." "It's like Japan."

Goto: **Ni⌐ppo⌐n to ni⌐te ima⌐su yo.** 日本と似ていますよ。

Kawa: "Something" **to nite imasu**, "be similar to something." Literally, "It resembles Japan." In the meantime, a new program begins on TV. Mrs. Ito warns him. "Look! It's a judo match." "A judo match" is **juudo no shiai**.

Goto: **A, ju⌐udoo no shi⌐ai de⌐su yo.** あ、柔道の試合ですよ。

Kawa: You can utter a voice of little exclamation: **A!** in place of "Look!" Listen again.

Goto: **A, ju⌐udoo no shi⌐ai de⌐su yo.** あ、柔道の試合ですよ。

Kawa: Mr. Smith notices that the match is between women.

Goto: **O⌐nna no hito⌐ desu ne.** 女の人ですね。

Kawa: A free translation would be: "That's between women, isn't it?"

Goto: **O⌐nna no hito⌐ desu ne.** 女の人ですね。

Kawa: Mrs. Ito's explanation in part: "In the past, only men used to do it, but..."

Goto: **Mu⌐kashi wa⌐ o⌐toko no hito ba⌐kari deshita ga.**
昔は男の人ばかりでしたが。

Kawa: That's our third key sentence, remember? she continues with: "nowadays, women have started doing it, too."

Goto: **Ko⌐nogoro wa⌐ o⌐nna no hito⌐ mo ya⌐ru yo⌐o ni na⌐rima⌐shita.**
このごろは女の人もやるようになりました。

Kawa: And this is our fourth key sentence. Now, you'll listen to the whole conversation again.

◆ **Today's Conversation**

I: **Su⌐misu-san no o⌐kuni de⌐ mo su⌐po⌐otsu sa⌐kan de⌐su ka.**
スミスさんのおくにでもスポーツさかんですか。

S: **E⌐e, fu⌐ttobo⌐oru ya ⌐te⌐nisu nado i⌐roiro arima⌐su. Jo⌐gingu o suru**

hito˥ mo ta⌐kusan ima˥su. Ni⌐ho˥n to ni⌐te ima˥su yo.
ええ、フットボールやテニスなどいろいろあります。ジョギングを
する人もたくさんいます。日本と似ていますよ。

I: **A, ju˥udoo no shi⌐ai de˥su yo.** あ、柔道の試合ですよ。

S: **O⌐nna no hito˥ desu ne.** 女の人ですね。

I: **Mu⌐kashi wa˥ o⌐toko no hito ba˥kari deshita ga, ko⌐nogoro wa˥ o⌐nna no hito˥ mo ya⌐ru yo˥o ni na⌐rima˥shita.**
昔は男の人ばかりでしたが、このごろは女の人もやるようになりま
した。

Kawa: You'll now review today's vocabulary. Please repeat aloud after Goto-san, who'll say each word or phrase twice. First, "old days."

Goto: **Mu⌐kashi.** 昔

Kawa: "Popular" or "flourishing."

Goto: **Sa⌐kan.** 盛ん

Kawa: "Be similar to."

Goto: **Ni⌐te ima˥su.** 似ています。

Kawa: Now, today's key sentences. This time, just listen to Goto-san. Today's first key sentence, "Is sport popular in your country, too, Mr. Smith?"

Goto: **Su˥misu-san no o⌐kuni de˥ mo su⌐po˥otsu ga sa⌐kan de˥su ka.**
スミスさんのおくにでもスポーツが盛んですか。

Kawa: The second key sentence: "They sell magazines, books and various other things."

Goto: **Za⌐sshi ya ho˥n nado o u⌐rima˥su.** 雑誌や本などを売ります。

Kawa: The third key sentence: "In the past, only men used to do it."

Goto: **Mu⌐kashi wa˥ o⌐toko no hito ba˥kari deshita.**
昔は男の人ばかりでした。

Kawa: The fourth key sentence, "Nowadays, women have started doing it, too."

Goto: **Ko⌐nogoro wa˥ o⌐nna no hito˥ mo ya⌐ru yo˥o ni na⌐rima˥shita.**
このごろは女の人もやるようになりました。

Kawa: Now, before we wind up, we have another chance to listen to the whole dialogue.

◆ **Today's Conversation**

I: **Su˥misu-san no o⌐kuni de˥ mo su⌐po˥otsu sa⌐kan de˥su ka.**
スミスさんのおくにでもスポーツさかんですか。

S: **E˥e, fu⌐ttobo˥oru ya ⌐te˥nisu nado i⌐roiro arima˥su. Jo⌐gingu o suru hito˥ mo ta⌐kusan ima˥su. Ni⌐ho˥n to ni⌐te ima˥su yo.**

ええ、フットボールやテニスなどいろいろあります。ジョギングを
する人もたくさんいます。日本と似ていますよ。

I: **A, ju⌐udoo no shi⌐ai de⌐su yo.** あ、柔道の試合ですよ。

S: **O⌐nna no hito⌐ desu ne.** 女の人ですね。

I: **Mu⌐kashi wa⌐ o⌐toko no hito ba⌐kari deshita ga, ko⌐nogoro wa⌐
o⌐nna no hito⌐ mo ya⌐ru yo⌐o ni na⌐rima⌐shita.**
昔は男の人ばかりでしたが、このごろは女の人もやるようになりま
した。

Notes

1. A ya B (ya C) nado ga arimasu.

A **ya** B **nado** (**ga**) a⌐rima⌐su. (There are A, B, and so on.)
A **ya** B **nado** (**o**) ka⌐ima⌐shita. (I bought such things as A and B.)
A **ya** B **nado** e i⌐kima⌐shita. (I went to such places as A, B, etc.)

Particle **ya** indicates that the list, "A and B," is a partial list. **Na⌐do** further emphasizes
"and other such things." Particles **ga** and **o** are sometimes lost when **nado** is used.

2. Ni⌐ppo⌐n ni ni⌐te ima⌐su yo.

The verb is **ni⌐ru**, but it is almost always used in the **ni⌐te iru** or **ni⌐ta** form to describe
similarity. X **ni ni⌐te iru** and X **to ni⌐te iru** can be used interchangeably without any
significant differences in meaning.

A⌐no onna⌐ no ko wa o⌐to⌐osan ni ni⌐te ima⌐su ne. ("That girl looks like her father,
doesn't she?")
Sa⌐kura ni nita hana⌐ ga miemasu. ("We can see flowers that resemble cherry
blossoms.")

3. ya⌐ru yo⌐o ni ⌐na⌐ru ("have come to do")

In Lesson 40 you learned the expression **ku⌐raku na⌐ru.** ("It gets dark.") The same verb
na⌐ru ("to become") appears above, indicating "a change to another stage." To
summarize the forms:

a) Adjective **-ku** form plus **naru** (**O⌐okiku naru.**)
b) Noun plus **ni** plus **naru** (**Se⌐nse⌐e ni naru.**)
c) Verb **-(r)u** form plus **yoo ni naru** (**Ha⌐nase⌐ru yoo ni naru.**) (**Yoo** is a noun meaning
"likeness.")

Additional Vocabulary

go⌐rufu	（ゴルフ）	golf
sa⌐kkaa	（サッカー）	soccer
ya⌐kyuu	（野球）	baseball

su⌐ki¬i	（スキー）	skiing
su⌐keeto	（スケート）	skating
su⌐iee	（水泳）	swimming
i¬ma	（今）	now
sa⌐kki	（さっき）	a while ago
mo⌐o su¬gu	（もうすぐ）	before long
kyo¬o	（今日）	today
ki⌐noo	（昨日）	yesterday
o⌐toto¬i	（おととい）	the day before yesterday
a⌐shita; a¬su	（明日）	tomorrow
a⌐sa¬tte	（あさって）	the day after tomorrow
ko⌐toshi	（今年）	this year
kyo¬nen	（去年）	last year
ra⌐inen	（来年）	next year
sa⌐rainen	（さ来年）	the year after next
mu⌐kashi	（昔）	in the past
ko⌐nogoro	（このごろ）	nowadays
i¬tsuka	（いつか）	someday

Exercises

1. Substitute the cue word for the underlined word in the model sentence.

   Model Sentence: **Su¬misu-san no o⌐kuni de¬ mo <u>su⌐po¬otsu</u> ga sa⌐kan de¬su ka.**

   1. te¬nisu
   2. su⌐iee
   3. ya⌐kyuu
   4. go¬rufu
   5. su⌐ki¬i
   6. ka⌐raoke
   7. pa⌐chinko

2. Following the example, construct sentences using **na¬do**.

   Example: **ho¬n; za⌐sshi; u⌐tte ima¬su→Ho¬n ya za⌐sshi na¬do o u⌐tte ima¬su.**

   1. Su¬misu-san; Sa⌐too-san; ki¬ma¬shita
   2. shi⌐nbun; za⌐sshi; ka⌐wana¬kereba narimasen
   3. Na¬ra; Kyo¬oto; i⌐kita¬i n desu
   4. Pa¬ri; Nyu⌐uyo¬oku; ra⌐inen iku so¬o desu
   5. E⌐ego; Fu⌐ransugo; ka⌐ite aru hon mo yo¬mema¬su
   6. su⌐ki¬i; su⌐iee; su⌐ki¬ desu
   7. te¬nisu; su⌐ki¬i; sa⌐kan de¬su
   8. ta⌐ma¬go; to¬osuto; ke¬sa ta⌐bema¬shita

3. Substitute the cue word or phrase for the underlined phrase in the model sentence.

Model Sentence: **Mu⌈kashi wa⌉ <u>o⌈toko no hito</u> ba⌈kari deshita.**

1. o⌈nna no hito
2. o⌈tona
3. ko⌈domo
4. ga⌈kusee
5. ha⌈taraite iru otoko no hito
6. wa⌈ka⌉i hito
7. ga⌈ikoku no hito
8. To⌈okyoo no hito
9. wa⌈ka⌉i o⌈nna no hito
10. Ni⌈honji⌉n

4. Substitute the cue for the underlined word in the model sentence.

Model Sentence: **Ko⌈nogoro wa⌉ o⌈nna no hito⌉ mo <u>ya⌈ru</u> yo⌉o ni na⌈rima⌉shita.**

1. so⌉to de ha⌈taraku
2. da⌈igaku e iku
3. ko⌈no shigoto o suru
4. ke⌈esatsu⌉kan (police officer) ni ⌈na⌉ru
5. ka⌈raoke o yaru
6. so⌉to de o⌈sake o no⌉mu
7. ta⌈bako o suu
8. ka⌈choo ya⌉ bu⌈choo na⌉do ni ⌈na⌉ru

5. Substitute the cue for both sections underlined in the model sentence.

Model Sentence: **Mu⌈kashi wa <u>ju⌉udoo o ya⌈ru⌉</u> no wa o⌈toko no hito ba⌈kari deshita ga, ko⌈nogoro wa⌉ o⌈nna no hito⌉ mo <u>ya⌈ru</u> yo⌉o ni na⌈rima⌉shita.**

1. so⌉to de ha⌈taraku
2. so⌉to de o⌈sake o no⌉mu
3. da⌈igaku e iku
4. ke⌈esatsu⌉kan ni ⌈na⌉ru
5. ko⌈no koojo⌉o de ha⌈taraku

6. Read the following dialogues and see if you understand them.

1. A: **Su⌈po⌉otsu wa o⌈suki de⌉su ka.**
   B: **E⌉e, mu⌈kashi wa te⌉nisu bakari deshita ga, ko⌈nogoro wa go⌈rufu mo ya⌈ru yo⌉o ni narimashita.**

A: Ja, iˈtsuka iˈssho ni goˈrufu yaˈrimashoˈo.

B: Eˈe, oˈnegai shimaˈsu.

2. A: Oˈkosan, oˈokiku ˈnaˈtta deshoo ne.

B: Eˈe, koˈnogoro wa kaˈnari haˈnaseˈru yoo ni narimashita. Oˈtaku wa?

A: Uˈe no ko wa kyoˈnen daˈigaku ni hairimaˈshita shi, shiˈta no ko moˈ raˈinen daigaku desˈu.

B: Soˈo desu ka. Iˈi desu ne. Uˈchi no ko wa maˈda ˈchiˈisakute taˈihen deˈsu yo.

3. A: Kiˈnooˈ aˈnoˈ aˈtarashiˈi resutoran e iˈtte mimaˈshita yo.

B: Aˈa, doˈo deshita ka.

A: Oˈishiˈkatta desu ga, choˈtto taˈkaˈi to omoimashita.

B: Yoˈoshoku deˈsu ka.

A: Iˈe, teˈnpura yaˈ saˈshimiˈ nado niˈhon-fuu no monoˈ ga ˈoˈokatta desu.

B: Waˈshoku waˈ taˈkaˈi desu kara ne. Koˈnde imashita ka.

A: Iˈe, juˈunin guˈrai deshita ga oˈnna no hito baˈkari deshita yo.

Answers

1. 1. Suˈmisu-san no oˈkuni deˈ mo, teˈnisu ga saˈkan deˈsu ka.
   2. Suˈmisu-san no oˈkuni deˈ mo, suˈiee ga sakan deˈsu ka.
   3. Suˈmisu-san no oˈkuni deˈ mo, yaˈkyuu ga sakan deˈsu ka.
   4. Suˈmisu-san no oˈkuni deˈ mo, goˈrufu ga saˈkan deˈsu ka.
   5. Suˈmisu-san no oˈkuni deˈ mo, suˈkiˈi ga saˈkan deˈsu ka.
   6. Suˈmisu-san no oˈkuni deˈ mo, kaˈraoke ga sakan deˈsu ka.
   7. Suˈmisu-san no oˈkuni deˈ mo, paˈchinko ga sakan deˈsu ka.

2. 1. Suˈmisu-san ya ˈSaˈtoo-san nado ga kiˈmaˈshita.
   2. Shiˈnbun yaˈ zaˈsshi naˈdo o kaˈwanaˈkereba narimasen.
   3. Naˈra ya ˈKyoˈoto nado e iˈkitaˈi n desu.
   4. Paˈri ya Nyuˈuyoˈoku nado e raˈinen iku soˈo desu.
   5. Eˈego ya Furansugo naˈdo de ˈkaˈite aru hon mo yoˈmemaˈsu.
   6. Suˈkiˈi ya suˈiee naˈdo ga suˈkiˈi desu.
   7. Teˈnisu ya suˈkiˈi nado ga saˈkan deˈsu.
   8. Taˈmaˈgo ya ˈtoˈosuto nado o ˈkeˈsa taˈbemaˈshita.

3. 1. Muˈkashi waˈ oˈnna no hito baˈkari deshita.
   2. Muˈkashi waˈ oˈtona baˈkari deshita.
   3. Muˈkashi waˈ koˈdomo baˈkari deshita.
   4. Muˈkashi waˈ gaˈkusee baˈkari deshita.
   5. Muˈkashi waˈ haˈtaraite iru otoko no hito baˈkari deshita.
   6. Muˈkashi waˈ waˈkaˈi hito ˈbaˈkari deshita.
   7. Muˈkashi waˈ gaˈikoku no hito baˈkari deshita.
   8. Muˈkashi waˈ Toˈokyoo no hito baˈkari deshita.
   9. Muˈkashi waˈ waˈkaˈi oˈnna no hito baˈkari deshita.
   10. Muˈkashi waˈ Niˈhonjiˈn ˈbaˈkari deshita.

4. 1. Koˈnogoro waˈ oˈnna no hitoˈ mo, soˈto de haˈtaraku yoˈo ni narimashita.
   2. Koˈnogoro waˈ oˈnna no hitoˈ mo, daˈigaku e iku yoˈo ni narimashita.

3. Ko⌐nogoro wa⌐ o⌐nna no hito⌐ mo, ko⌐no shigoto o suru yo⌐o ni narimashita.
4. Ko⌐nogoro wa⌐ o⌐nna no hito⌐ mo, ke⌐esatsu⌐kan ni ⌐na⌐ru yoo ni narimashita.
5. Ko⌐nogoro wa⌐ o⌐nna no hito⌐ mo, ka⌐raoke o yaru yo⌐o ni na⌐rima⌐shita.
6. Ko⌐nogoro wa⌐ o⌐nna no hito⌐ mo, so⌐to de o⌐sake o no⌐mu yoo ni narimashita.
7. Ko⌐nogoro wa⌐ o⌐nna no hito⌐ mo, ta⌐bako o suu yo⌐o ni narimashita.
8. Ko⌐nogoro wa⌐ o⌐nna no hito⌐ mo, ka⌐choo ya⌐ bu⌐choo na⌐do ni ⌐na⌐ru yoo ni na⌐rima⌐sita.

5. 1. Mu⌐kashi wa so⌐to de hataraku no wa o⌐toko no hito ba⌐kari deshita ga, ko⌐nogoro wa⌐ o⌐nna no hito⌐ mo ⌐so⌐to de ha⌐taraku yo⌐o ni narimashita.

2. Mu⌐kashi wa so⌐to de o⌐sake o no⌐mu no wa o⌐toko no hito ba⌐kari deshita ga, ko⌐nogoro wa⌐ o⌐nna no hito⌐ mo ⌐no⌐mu yoo ni narimashita.

3. Mu⌐kashi wa⌐ da⌐igaku e iku⌐ no wa o⌐toko no hito ba⌐kari deshita ga, ko⌐nogoro wa⌐ o⌐nna no hito⌐ mo da⌐igaku e iku yo⌐o ni narimashita.

4. Mu⌐kashi wa⌐ ke⌐esatsu⌐kan ni ⌐na⌐ru no wa o⌐toko no hito ba⌐kari deshita ga, ko⌐nogoro wa⌐ o⌐nna no hito mo ke⌐esatsu⌐kan ni ⌐na⌐ru yoo ni narimashita.

5. Mu⌐kashi wa⌐ ko⌐no koojo⌐o de hataraku no wa o⌐toko no hito ba⌐kari deshita ga, ko⌐nogoro wa⌐ o⌐nna no hito mo ha⌐taraku yoo ni narimashita.

6. 1. A: Do you like sports?
   B: Yes, I used to play just tennis in the past, but recently I've become a golfer, too.
   A: Well then, let's play golf together sometime.
   B: Yes, I'd love to.

2. A: Your children must have grown.
   B: Yes, she has gotten to be able to talk quite a bit these days. How about yours?
   A: The older one entered university last year; the younger one will also be in college next year.
   B: I see. That's really nice. Our kid is still small and requires a lot of work from us.

3. A: We tried that new restaurant yesterday.
   B: Oh? How was it?
   A: (The food) was good, but I thought it was a little expensive.
   B: Western food?
   A: No, they had many Japanese-style foods like tempura, sashimi, and so on.
   B: Japanese food is expensive, so.... Was it crowded?
   A: No. There were about ten people, but they were all women!

LESSON 44

DE⌈PA⌉ATO E IKU
デパートへ行く
Going to a Department Store

Today's Conversation

Smith: **Ko⌈ko ga⌉ ba⌈agen-se⌉eru no ka⌈ijoo de⌉su ka.**
ここがバーゲンセールの会場ですか。
Is this where the bargain sale is being held?

Ito: **E⌉e, ko⌉nde imasu ne. A, a⌈shi⌉ o fu⌈marenai yo⌉o ki ⌈o tsuke⌉te…**
ええ、こんでいますね。あ、足をふまれないよう気をつけて…
Yes. It's crowded, isn't it? Oh, watch out that no one steps on your feet.

Smith: **Ko⌈domo ga⌉ ta⌈kusan ima⌉su ne.**
子供がたくさんいますね。
There are many children, aren't there?

Ito: **Ni⌈chiyo⌉obi desu kara ko⌈domo ga o⌉oi n desu yo.**
日曜日ですから子供が多いんですよ。
Yes, there are. That's because it's Sunday today.

Smith: **A, ko⌈tchi⌉ wa ⌈na⌉n desu ka.**
あ、こっちは何ですか。
What are they doing?

Ito: **Ki⌉ngyo o tsu⌈ru⌉ n desu. Ya⌈tte mima⌉su ka.**
金魚をつるんです。やってみますか。
They are fishing for goldfish. Would you like to try?

Smith:	E⌐e. Mu⌐zukashi⌐i desu yo.
	ええ。むずかしいですよ。
	Yes…. Oh, this is difficult.
Ito:	A, ni⌐gerarema⌐shita ne.
	あ、逃げられましたね。
	It got away.
Smith:	I⌐to ga ki⌐rema⌐shita.
	糸が切れました。
	The line has snapped.

DEPAATO E IKU
デパートへ行く
Going to a Department Store

Kawa: Today, in Lesson 44, Mrs. Ito takes Mr. Smith to a department store. They go up to the roof of the store, where children are fishing for goldfish. Mr. Smith joins them to try it himself. But he finds it awfully hard to catch one. "Oh, it got away. The line has snapped." Our first key sentence is, "The goldfish got away." "Goldfish" is **kingyo**. "Get away," **nigeru**.

Goto: **Ki⌐ngyo ni ni⌐gerarema⌐shita.** 金魚に逃げられました。

Kawa: It practically means "The goldfish got away." But putting it more literally, **kingyo ni** in the context means "by the goldfish." The whole idea is that the speaker, Mrs. Ito, is sorry about what's happened to Mr. Smith as a result of trying to catch the fish. **Nige-raremashita** literally means "you had it escaped." This form **-raremashita**, as in the following examples, suggests the sense of loss on the speaker's part, the sense that you are the victim of something unfavorable or undesirable, which has taken place. How about a thief? "A thief" is **doroboo**. "A thief broke into my house" or, more literally, "I had my house broken into by a thief." "Break into," **hairu**, which is changed to **hairaremasu**, "to get something [like your house] broken into." And its past form is **hairaremashita**.

Goto: **Do⌐roboo ni⌐ ha⌐irarema⌐shita.** 泥棒にはいられました。

Kawa: Next, you want to say that it suddenly rained, and you got soaked wet. "Rain" is **ame**. Let's use the same pattern, **-raremashita**.

Goto: **A⌐me ni fu⌐rarema⌐shita.** 雨に降られました。

Kawa: Literally, "I was rained on." Our second key sentence is rather similar to the previous expression, **-raremashita**. "I got my feet trodden on." "Step on" is **fumu**.

Goto: **A⌈shi⌉ o fu⌈marema⌉shita.** 足をふまれました。

Kawa: **Fumu** has been changed to **fumaremashita**. "I got my feet trodden on," once again.

Goto: **A⌈shi⌉ o fu⌈marema⌉shita.** 足をふまれました。

Kawa: Next, "I had my purse stolen." "Purse" is **saifu**; "steal," **toru**.

Goto: **Sa⌈ifu o⌉ to⌈rarema⌉shita.** 財布をとられました。

Kawa: Now, what's the expression for this: You have arrived back in Japan and you're going to collect your baggage but have found your baggage is missing. Maybe someone took your baggage by mistake. "Someone has got my baggage because he took mine for his." "Baggage" is **nimotsu**; "take something for something else," **machigaeru**, which by itself means "make a mistake."

Goto: **Ni⌉motsu o ma⌈chigaerarema⌉shita.** 荷物を間違えられました。

Kawa: "Someone took my baggage by mistake." Our third key sentence is, "Mind your feet don't get trodden on." "Mind" in this context is **ki o tsukeru**.

Goto: **A⌈shi⌉o fu⌈marenai yo⌉o ni ki ⌈o tsuke⌉te kudasai.**
足をふまれないように気をつけて下さい。

Kawa: …**yooni ki o tsukeru**, which corresponds to "take good care of something so as to" or "in order that…." This pattern is often used in negative sentences as in the example, **fumare nai yoo ni**, "so as not to be stepped on."

Goto: **A⌈shi⌉o fu⌈marenai yo⌉o ni ki ⌈o tsuke⌉te kudasai.**
足をふまれないように気をつけて下さい。

Kawa: Now for a few substitutions. "Mind you don't break it." "Break," **kowasu**.

Goto: **Ko⌈wasa⌉nai yoo ni ki ⌈o tsuke⌉te kudasai.**
こわさないように気をつけて下さい。

Kawa: Next, "Mind you won't be taken ill." "Fall ill" is **byooki ni naru**.

Goto: **Byo⌈oki ni nara⌉nai yoo ni ki ⌈o tsuke⌉te kudasai.**
病気にならないように気をつけて下さい。

♪ **Station Break**〰〰〰〰〰〰〰〰〰〰〰〰〰〰〰〰〰〰〰〰〰

Kawa: Now, in the second half of this session, we'll discuss each dialogue. Listen to their conversation first.

◆ **Today's Conversation**

S: Ko⌐ko ga⌐ ba⌐agen-se⌐eru no ka⌐ijoo de⌐su ka.
ここがバーゲンセールの会場ですか。

I: E⌐e, ko⌐nde imasu ne. A, a⌐shi⌐ o fu⌐marenai yo⌐o ki ⌐o tsuke⌐te....
ええ、こんでいますね。あ、足をふまれないよう気をつけて....

S: Ko⌐domo ga⌐ ta⌐kusan ima⌐su ne.　子供がたくさんいますね。

I: Ni⌐chiyo⌐obi desu kara ko⌐domo ga o⌐oi n desu yo.
日曜日ですから子供が多いんですよ。

S: A, ko⌐tchi⌐ wa ⌐na⌐n desu ka.　あ、こっちは何ですか。

I: Ki⌐ngyo o tsu⌐ru⌐ n desu. Ya⌐tte mima⌐su ka.
金魚をつるんです。やってみますか。

S: E⌐e.... Mu⌐zukashi⌐i desu yo.　ええ。むずかしいですよ。

I: A, ni⌐gerarema⌐shita ne.　あ、逃げられましたね。

S: I⌐to ga ki⌐rema⌐shita.　糸が切れました。

Kawa: Next, you'll listen to its English version.

◆ **Same Conversation in English**

S: Is this where the bargain sale is being held?

I: Yes. It's crowded, isn't it? Oh, watch out that no one steps on your feet.

S: There are many children, aren't there?

I: Yes, there are. That's because it's Sunday today.

S: What are they doing?

I: They are fishing for goldfish. Would you like to try?

S: Yes.... Oh, this is difficult.

I: It got away.

S: The line has snapped.

Kawa: Now each dialogue. We start with the scene of bargain sales. Mr. Smith looks interested. "Is this where the bargain sales are being held?"

Goto: Ko⌐ko ga⌐ ba⌐agen-se⌐eru no ka⌐ijoo de⌐su ka.
ここがバーゲンセールの会場ですか。

Kawa: **Kaijoo** means "a site," "the place of an event," and so on. So **baagen-seeru no kaijoo** literally means "the site of bargain sales." It's naturally crowded there.

Goto: E⌐e, ko⌐nde imasu ne. ええ、こんでいますね。

Kawa: She said, "Yes. It's crowded, isn't it?" **Komu,** meaning "to be crowded," is changed to **konde imasu**, "it's crowded." **-te imasu** or **-de imasu** form shows the state of something.

Goto: **E⌐e, ko⌐nde imasu ne.** ええ、こんでいますね。

Kawa: You heard the third key sentence, "Mind your feet don't get trodden on."

Goto: **A, a⌐shi⌐ o fu⌐marenai yo⌐o ki ⌐o tsuke⌐te....**
あ、足をふまれないよう気をつけて....

Kawa: After awhile they go up to the roof, where there are many children playing around. "There are a lot of children, aren't there?" says Mr. Smith.

Goto: **Ko⌐domo ga⌐ ta⌐kusan ima⌐su ne.** 子供がたくさんいますね。

Kawa: "Yes, there are. That's because it's Sunday today," explains Mrs. Ito.

Goto: **Ni⌐chiyo⌐obi desu kara ko⌐domo ga o⌐oi n desu yo.**
日曜日ですから子供が多いんですよ。

Kawa: **Nichiyoobi** means "Sunday;" **nichiyoobi desu kara**, "because it's Sunday today." Suddenly, Mr. Smith is interested in what the children are doing near him. He asks, "Oh, what's this over here?"

Goto: **A, ko⌐tchi⌐ wa ⌐na⌐n desu ka.** あ、こっちは何ですか。

Kawa: **Kotchi** you've just heard is an informal word for **kochira**, "this over here." Mrs. Ito says, "They're fishing for goldfish. Would you like to try?"

Goto: **Ki⌐ngyo o tsu⌐ru⌐ n desu. Ya⌐tte mima⌐su ka.**
金魚をつるんです。やってみますか。

Kawa: **Kingyo** means "goldfish;" **yatte mimasu ka** is an idiomatic expression meaning "Would you like to try?" Mr. Smith would like to try and says **ee** or "yes." **Ee** is an informal expression for "yes." But he soon finds it's awfully difficult.

Goto: **Mu⌐zukashi⌐i desu yo.** むずかしいですよ。

Kawa: **Muzukashii** means "difficult." He tries hard but fails again. "It got away," comments Mrs. Ito.

Goto: **A, ni⌐gerarema⌐shita ne.** あ、逃げられましたね。

Kawa: **Nigeraremashita** is the main part of the first key sentence, denoting in the context the sense of loss. The short **a** is like "oh" in English. The fish got away, and besides, the line has snapped. "Line" is **ito**; "snapped," **kiremashita**.

Goto: **I⌐to ga ki⌐rema⌐shita.** 糸が切れました。

Kawa: Let's now listen to the whole conversation again.

◆ **Today's Conversation**

S: **Ko⌐ko ga⌐ ba⌐agen-se⌐eru no ka⌐ijoo de⌐su ka.**
ここがバーゲンセールの会場ですか。

I: E⌐e, ko⌐nde imasu ne. A, a⌐shi⌐ o fu⌐marenai yo⌐o ki ⌐o tsuke⌐te....
えゝ、こんでいますね。あ、足をふまれないよう気をつけて....

S: Ko⌐domo ga⌐ ta⌐kusan ima⌐su ne.　子供がたくさんいますね。

I: Ni⌐chiyo⌐obi desu kara ko⌐domo ga o⌐oi n desu yo.
日曜日ですから子供が多いんですよ。

S: A, ko⌐tchi⌐ wa ⌐na⌐n desu ka.　あ、こっちは何ですか。

I: Ki⌐ngyo o tsu⌐ru⌐ n desu. Ya⌐tte mima⌐su ka.
金魚をつるんです。やってみますか。

S: E⌐e. Mu⌐zukashi⌐i desu yo.　えゝ。むずかしいですよ。

I: A, ni⌐gerema⌐shita ne.　あ、逃げられましたね。

S: I⌐to ga ki⌐rema⌐shita.　糸が切れました。

Kawa: Next, as usual, you'll practice today's vocabulary. Please repeat aloud after Goto-san, who will say each word or phrase twice. First, "foot."

Goto: A⌐shi⌐.　足

Kawa: "Watch out" or "take care."

Goto: Ki ⌐o tsuke⌐ru.　気をつける。

Kawa: "Here;" "this side."

Goto: Ko⌐tchi⌐.　こっち

Kawa: "Escape;" "get away."

Goto: Ni⌐ge⌐ru.　逃げる。

Kawa: Now the key sentences again. This time, just listen to Goto-san. The first key sentence: "The goldfish got away" or, literally, "You had the goldfish escaped."

Goto: Ki⌐ngyo ni ni⌐gerarema⌐shita.　金魚に逃げられました。

Kawa: Next, the second key sentence, "I've got my foot trodden on."

Goto: A⌐shi⌐ o fu⌐marema⌐shita.　足をふまれました。

Kawa: And the third key sentence, "Mind your feet don't get trodden on."

Goto: A⌐shi⌐o fu⌐marenai yo⌐o ni ki ⌐o tsuke⌐te kudasai.
足をふまれないように気をつけて下さい。

Kawa: Now, you'll listen to their conversation again.

◆ **Today's Conversation**

S: Ko⌐ko ga⌐ ba⌐agen-se⌐eru no ka⌐ijoo de⌐su ka.
ここがバーゲンセールの会場ですか。

I: E⌐e, ko⌐nde imasu ne. A, a⌐shi⌐ o fu⌐marenai yo⌐o ki ⌐o tsuke⌐te....
えゝ、こんでいますね。あ、足をふまれないよう気をつけて....

S: Ko⌐domo ga⌐ ta⌐kusan ima⌐su ne.　子供がたくさんいますね。

I: **Ni⌈chi-yo⌉obi desu kara ko⌈domo ga o⌉oi n desu yo.**
　　日曜日ですから子供が多いんですよ。

S: **A, ko⌈tchi⌉ wa ⌈na⌉n desu ka.**　あ、こっちは何ですか。

I: **Ki⌉ngyo o tsu⌈ru⌉ n desu. Ya⌈tte mima⌉su ka.**
　　金魚をつるんです。やってみますか。

S: **E⌉e. Mu⌈zukashi⌉i desu yo.**　ええ。むずかしいですよ。

I: **A, ni⌈gerarema⌉shita ne.**　あ、逃げられましたね。

S: **I⌉to ga ki⌈rema⌉shita.**　糸が切れました。

Notes

1. A⌈shi⌉ o fu⌈marenai yo⌉o (ni) ki ⌈o tsuke⌉te (kudasai).

There are many idiomatic expressions with the word **ki** ("spirit," "mind," "feeling"), and **ki⌈o tsuke⌉ru** is one of them, meaning "pay attention," "watch out." **Ku⌈ruma ni ki o tsuke⌉te kudasai.** ("Watch out for cars.")

-yo⌉o (ni) ki ⌈o tsuke⌉ru or "to look out so that…" is more often used with a verb in the negative form: "Be careful, so that you won't.…"

2. Ko⌈tchi⌉ wa nan desu ka.

Ko⌈tchi⌉ is the informal, conversational equivalent of **kochira.**

Also learn:

ko⌈tchi	**(ko⌈chira)**
so⌈tchi⌉	**(so⌈chira)**
a⌈tchi⌉	**(a⌈chira)**
do⌈tchi	**(do⌈chira)**

3. Ni⌈gerarema⌉shita ne.

-(r)a⌈re is the Japanese passive form. This form is used to express the passive meaning, as in **ko⌈rosaremashita**, "he was killed" ("to kill:" **ko⌈rosu**). The passive form is perhaps used more often, however, to show the speaker's annoyance with what has happened. If, for instance, your cat ate your pet goldfish, **ta⌈berarema⌉shita**, the passive form would be used. The subject of this passive verb, however, is not the goldfish but the speaker, "I." So, in English it would read: "I had my pet goldfish eaten by my cat." Yet since this construction also implies your annoyance with what has occurred, another English version of this sentence could read: "My cat ate my pet goldfish, and I was upset."

A⌉me ga fu⌈rima⌉shita. ("It rained.") is an objective and neutral statement. **A⌉me ni fu⌈rarema⌉shita.** ("I was rained on."), however, implies that the speaker felt negatively toward the rainfall.

The passive form of **su⌐ru** is **sa⌐reru**. **Ku⌐ru** becomes **ko⌐rareru**.

Note that the subject marking **ga** changes to **ni** ("by") in the -**ra⌐reru** pattern.

Additional Vocabulary

te⌐	(手)	hand; arm
a⌐ta⌐ma	(頭)	head
ka⌐o	(顔)	face
me⌐	(目)	eyes
ha⌐na	(鼻)	nose
ku⌐chi	(口)	mouth
ha⌐	(歯)	teeth
mi⌐mi⌐	(耳)	ears
o⌐naka	(お腹)	stomach; abdomen
ni⌐motsu	(荷物)	baggage; belongings
sa⌐ifu	(さいふ)	wallet
do⌐roboo	(どろぼう)	thief
nu⌐su⌐mu	(ぬすむ)	steal
ma⌐chigae⌐ru	(まちがえる)	make a mistake
a⌐me ga ⌐fu⌐ru	(雨がふる)	rain falls
byo⌐oki ni na⌐ru	(病気になる)	become ill
i⌐ta⌐i	(痛い)	painful
ko⌐wa⌐su	(こわす)	break
o⌐to⌐su	(落とす)	drop; lose

Exercises

1. Substitute the cue word for the word underlined in the model sentence.

   Model sentence: <u>A⌐shi⌐</u> ga i⌐ta⌐i n desu. ("My feet hurt.")

   1. a⌐ta⌐ma
   2. te⌐
   3. me⌐
   4. mi⌐mi⌐
   5. o⌐naka
   6. ha⌐na
   7. ku⌐chi
   8. ha⌐

2. Passive form. Change each verb first to its negative form, then put it into the passive, according to the example.

   Example: ta⌐be⌐ru; ta⌐be⌐nai; ta⌐berare⌐ru
   no⌐mu; no⌐ma⌐nai; no⌐mare⌐ru

1. fu⌐mu   ("to step on")
2. to⌐ru   ("to take," "steal")
3. yu⌐u   ("to say")
4. nu⌐su⌐mu   ("to steal")
5. fu⌐ru   ("to rain;" "to snow")
6. ha⌐iru   ("to get in")
7. ni⌐ge⌐ru   ("to escape")
8. mi⌐ru   ("to look at")
9. su⌐ru   ("to do")
10. ku⌐ru   ("to come")

3. Express the following sentences in passive.

   Example: Ki⌐ngyo ga ni⌐ge⌐ru→Ki⌐ngyo ni ni⌐gerare⌐ru.

   1. Do⌐roboo ga ha⌐iru.
   2. Hi⌐to ga mi⌐ru.
   3. A⌐me ga ⌐fu⌐ru.
   4. To⌐modachi ga ku⌐ru.
   5. Do⌐roboo ga nusu⌐mu.
   6. Do⌐roboo ga nige⌐ru.

4. Express the following sentences in past-tense passive.

   Example: A⌐shi⌐ o fu⌐mu→A⌐shi⌐ o fu⌐marema⌐shita.

   1. Ni⌐motsu o ⌐to⌐ru.
   2. Na⌐mae o machiga⌐eru.
   3. Ka⌐o o mi⌐ru.
   4. Sa⌐ifu o to⌐ru.
   5. Ka⌐ban o nusu⌐mu.

5. -yo⌐o ni ki ⌐o tsuke⌐te kudasai

Following the example, use the cue word or phrase to construct sentences that mean "Please be careful so as not to…."

   Example: ma⌐chigae⌐ru→Ma⌐chigae⌐nai yoo ni ki ⌐o tsuke⌐te kudasai.

   1. o⌐soku na⌐ru
   2. ko⌐wa⌐su
   3. byo⌐oki ni na⌐ru
   4. fu⌐mu
   5. o⌐to⌐su
   6. ni⌐motsu o to⌐rare⌐ru
   7. ka⌐ban o nusumare⌐ru
   8. sa⌐ifu o torare⌐ru

9. aˈshiˈ o fuˈmareru
10. doˈroboo ni hairareˈru

6. Do you understand the following dialogues?

1. A: Kiˈnooˈ deˈkaketaˈ n desu ga, aˈme ni fuˈraremaˈshita yo.
   B: Soˈre wa taihen deˈshita ne. Aˈsa, ˈiˈi ˈteˈnki datta n desu ga ne.

2. A: Zuˈibun konde imasu ne.
   B: Eˈe, aˈshiˈ o fuˈmarenai yoˈo ni ki ˈo tsukeˈte.

3. A: Suˈzuki-san, kiˈnooˈ doˈroboo ni hairaˈreta soo desu yo.
   B: Soˈo desu ka. Naˈni o toˈraˈreta n desu ka.

   A: Oˈkane ya kaˈmera ya taˈkaˈi ˈeˈ nado o nuˈsumaˈreta soo desu.
   B: Taˈihen deˈshita ne. Doˈroboo ni hairareˈnai yoo ni ki ˈo tsukemashoˈo.

Answers

1. 1. Aˈtaˈma ga iˈtaˈi n desu.
   2. Teˈ ga iˈtaˈi n desu.
   3. Meˈ ga iˈtaˈi n desu.
   4. Miˈmiˈ ga iˈtaˈi n desu.
   5. Oˈnaka gaˈ iˈtaˈi n desu.
   6. Haˈna gaˈ iˈtaˈi n desu.
   7. Kuˈchi gaˈ iˈtaˈi n desu.
   8. Haˈ ga iˈtaˈi n desu.

2. 1. fuˈmareru
   2. toˈrareˈru
   3. iˈwareru
   4. nuˈsumareˈru
   5. fuˈrareˈru
   6. haˈirareˈru
   7. niˈgerareˈru
   8. miˈrareˈru
   9. saˈreru
   10. koˈrareˈru

3. 1. Doˈroboo ni hairareˈru.
   2. Hiˈto ni mirareˈru.
   3. Aˈme ni fuˈrareˈru.
   4. Toˈmodachi ni korareˈru.
   5. Doˈroboo ni nusumareˈru.
   6. Doˈroboo ni nigerareˈru.

4. 1. Niˈmotsu o toˈraremaˈshita.
   2. Naˈmae o machigaeraremaˈshita.
   3. Kaˈo o miraremaˈshita.
   4. Saˈifu o toraremaˈshita.
   5. Kaˈban o nusumaremaˈshita.

5. 1. O⌐soku nara⌐nai yoo ni ki ⌐o tsuke⌐te kudasai.
   2. Kowasa⌐nai yoo ni ki ⌐o tsuke⌐te kudasai.
   3. Byo⌐oki ni nara⌐nai yoo ni ki ⌐o tsuke⌐te kudasai.
   4. Fu⌐manai yo⌐o ni ki ⌐o tsuke⌐te kudasai.
   5. O⌐tosa⌐nai yoo ni ki ⌐o tsuke⌐te kudasai.
   6. Ni⌐motsu o to⌐rare⌐nai yoo ni ki ⌐o tsuke⌐te kudasai.
   7. Ka⌐ban o nusumare⌐nai yoo ni ki ⌐o tsuke⌐te kudasai.
   8. Sa⌐ifu o torare⌐nai yoo ni ki ⌐o tsuke⌐te kudasai.
   9. A⌐shi⌐ o fu⌐marenai yo⌐o ni ki ⌐o tsuke⌐te kudasai.
   10. Do⌐roboo ni hairare⌐nai yoo ni ki ⌐o tsuke⌐te kudasai.

6. 1. A: I went out yesterday, but I was rained on.
      B: That was too bad. The weather was fine in the morning, though, wasn't it?

   2. A: It's awfully crowded, isn't it?
      B: Yes, be careful so no one steps on your feet.

   3. A: Mr. Suzuki had his house entered by a thief.
      B: Is that right? What was stolen?

      A: Money, cameras, expensive paintings, and so on, they told me.
      B: That's too bad. Let's take care that no thieves break in.

NIᴦPPON NO SHUUKAN NO HANASHI
日本の習慣の話
Talking about Japanese Customs

Today's Conversation

Smith: **Oᴵkusan no shigoto wa taᴦihen deᴵsu ne.**
奥さんの仕事は大変ですね。
Housewives have lots of things to do, haven't they?

Ito: **Eᴵe, iᴦsogashiᴵi desu ᴦneᴵe.**
ええ、忙しいですねえ。
Yes, we are very busy.

Smith: **Iᴵtsu ga iᴦchibanᴵ iᴦsogashiᴵi desu ka.**
いつが一番忙しいですか。
When's the busiest time for you?

Ito: **Oᴦshoogatsuᴵ desu ne. Muᴦkashi waᴵ oᴦmochi o tsuᴵitari, toᴦkubetsu no ryoᴵori o tsuᴦkuᴵttari suru node, toᴦtemo taihen deᴵshita. Uᴦchi no naᴵka mo soᴦoji shite okanaᴵkereba naᴦraᴵnai shi.**
お正月ですね。昔はおもちをついたり、特別の料理を作ったりするので、とても大変でした。うちの中も掃除しておかなければならないし。
The New Year season. We used to do a great deal: pounding rice cakes, cooking special dishes and cleaning the house.

Smith: **Koᴦnogoro waᴵ soᴦre hodo deᴵ mo ᴦnaᴵi n desu ka.**
このごろはそれほどでもないんですか。
So you don't have to do so much these days?

Ito:	E⌐e, o⌐mochi mo⌐ sho⌐ogatu-yoo no ryo⌐ori mo mi⌐se⌐ de ka⌐ema⌐su kara ne. ええ、おもちも正月用の料理も店で買えますからね。 No. We can buy rice cakes and special dishes at stores.

NIPPON NO SHUUKAN NO HANASHI
日本の習慣の話
Talking about Japanese Customs

Kawa: Today, in Lesson 45, Mr. Smith asks Mrs. Ito about Japanese customs. She tells him housewives in Japan get busiest in the New Year season. It used to be particularly so in the old days. For instance, they had to clean up the inside of the house thoroughly. Our first key sentence is, "We have to clean up the inside of the house." "To clean up" is **sooji shimasu**.

Goto: **So⌐oji shite okana⌐kereba na⌐rimase⌐n.**
掃除しておかなければなりません。

Kawa: You may have noticed "the inside of the house," **uchi no naka**, is missing. You are right. But let's ignore it just for now. Here, we'll learn the pattern **-te okanakereba narimasen**, "must finish doing something in advance." **Sooji shite** is the -te form of **sooji shimasu**, "to clean up." **Sooji shite okanakereba narimasen** means "We must clean up something" well ahead to be ready for what's forthcoming. In this case, something must be cleaned up in perfect order before the New Year.

Goto: **So⌐oji shite okana⌐kereba na⌐rimase⌐n.**
掃除しておかなければなりません。

Kawa: Now a few substitutions. "We must make reservation beforehand." "To make reservation" is **yoyaku shimasu**.

Goto: **Yo⌐yaku shite okana⌐kereba na⌐rimase⌐n.**
予約しておかなければなりません。

Kawa: How about **denwa o kakemasu**, "to telephone." "We must make a phone call in advance."

Goto: **De⌐nwa o ka⌐kete o⌐kana⌐kereba na⌐rimase⌐n.**
電話をかけておかなければなりません。

Kawa: You'll have one more. "We must prepare dishes ready well ahead." "To prepare dishes," **ryoori o tsukurimasu**.

Goto: **Ryo⌐ori o tsu⌐ku⌐tte okanakereba na⌐rimase⌐n.**
料理を作っておかなければなりません。

Kawa: Next, the second key sentence that features **-tari…-tari**, which may be similar to those of English patterns used for phrases such as "now standing and now sitting," "what with flattery and what with force," and so on. Here, we deal with "pounding rice cakes," **omochi o tsukimasu**, and "cooking special dishes," **tokubetsu no ryoori o tsukurimasu**. "We used to pound rice cakes and cook special dishes. So there was a lot of work to do."

Goto: **O⌐mochi tsu⌐itari, to⌐kubetsu no ryo⌐ori o tsu⌐ku⌐ttari suru node ta⌐ihen de⌐shita.**
おもちをついたり、特別の料理を作ったりするので、大変でした。

Kawa: **Omochi o tsuitari**, "what with pounding rice cakes;" **tokubetsu no ryoori o tsukuttari**, "and what with cooking special dishes." **Taihen** itself means "tough," "not easy," "of no small consideration," etc., but **taihen deshita** in this context means "there was a lot of work to do." Listen to Goto-san again.

Goto: **O⌐mochi o tsu⌐itari, to⌐kubetsu no ryo⌐ori o tsu⌐ku⌐ttari suru node ta⌐ihen de⌐shita.**
おもちをついたり、特別の料理を作ったりするので、大変でした。

Kawa: Let's have a few substitutions now. "There was a lot of work to do, now cleaning up the house, and now cooking dishes."

Goto: **So⌐oji o shita⌐ri, ryo⌐ori o tsu⌐ku⌐ttari su⌐ru⌐ node, ta⌐ihen de⌐shita.**
掃除をしたり、料理を作ったりするので、大変でした。

Kawa: What about this one: "I had a lot to do then, working and studying alternately."

Goto: **Shi⌐goto o shita⌐ri, be⌐nkyo o shita⌐ri su⌐ru⌐ node ta⌐ihen de⌐shita.**
仕事をしたり、勉強をしたりするので、大変でした。

Kawa: So far, we've only dealt with hard work, but you can use the pattern for something much more pleasant as well. For example, "We really had a nice time going to the movies [cinema] and then to a coffeehouse." "To go to the movies," **eega o mimasu**; "to go to a coffeehouse," **kissaten ni hairimasu**. "Had a very good time," **totemo tanoshikatta desu**.

Goto: **E⌐ega o ⌐mi⌐tari, ki⌐ssa⌐ten ni ⌐ha⌐ittarishite, to⌐temo tanoshi⌐katta desu.**
映画を見たり、喫茶店に入ったりして、とても楽しかったです。

Kawa: "We had a very good time going to the movies and then to a coffeehouse."

♪ **Station Break** ‖‖‖

Kawa: In the second half of this program, we'll discuss each dialogue as usual. Listen to the whole conversation first.

◆ **Today's Conversation**

S: Oˈkusan no shigoto wa taˈihen deˈsu ne.
奥さんの仕事は大変ですね。

I: Eˈe, iˈsogashiˈi desu ˈneˈe. ええ、忙しいですねえ。

S: Iˈtsu ga iˈchibanˈ iˈsogashiˈi desu ka. いつが一番忙しいですか。

I: Oˈshoogatsuˈ desu ne. Muˈkashi waˈ oˈmochi o tsuˈitari, toˈkubetsu no ryoˈori o tsuˈkuˈttari suru node, toˈtemo taihen deˈshita. Uˈchi no naˈka mo soˈoji shite okanaˈkereba naˈraˈnai shi.
お正月ですね。昔はおもちをついたり、特別の料理を作ったりするので、とても大変でした。うちの中も掃除しておかなければならないし。

S: Koˈnogoro waˈ soˈre hodo deˈ mo ˈnaˈi n desu ka.
このごろはそれほどでもないんですか。

I: Eˈe, oˈmochi moˈ shoˈogatu-yoo no ryoˈori mo miˈseˈ de kaˈemaˈsu kara ne.
ええ、おもちも正月用の料理も店で買えますからね。

Kawa: Next, you'll listen to its English version.

◆ **Same Conversation in English**

S: Housewives have lots of things to do, haven't they?
I: Yes, we are very busy.
S: When's the busiest time for you?
I: The New Year season. We used to do a great deal: pounding rice cakes, cooking special dishes and cleaning the house.
S: So you don't have to do so much these days?
I: No. We can buy rice cakes and special dishes at stores.

Kawa: Now we study each dialogue. Mr. Smith thinks that Japanese housewives are pretty busy. He says, "Housewives have lots of things to do, haven't they?

Goto: Oˈkusan no shigoto wa taˈihen deˈsu ne.
奥さんの仕事は大変ですね。

Kawa: **Okusan** itself usually means someone's "wife" or "Mrs. So-and-so," when you're speaking to her. But here, it refers to "Japanese housewives" in general. **Shigoto** is "work." **Okusan no shigoto** here means "the work of housewives in Japan." I hope you remember the use of **taihen**, which is part of the second key sentence. Mrs. Ito agrees with him. "Yes, we are very busy." "Busy" is **isogashii**.

Goto: Eˈe, iˈsogashiˈi desu ˈneˈe. ええ、忙しいですねえ。

Kawa: Mr. Smith would like to know when they are busiest. He asks, "When's the busiest time for you?"

Goto: I⌈tsu ga i⌈chiban⌉ i⌈sogashi⌉i desu ka.　いつが一番忙しいですか。

Kawa: **Itsu** means "when;" **ichiban**, "most." **Ichiban isogashii**, "busiest." "It's the New Year," says Mrs. Ito. She continues, "In the old days, we used to pound rice cakes and cook special dishes. So there was a lot of work to do. We also had to clean up the inside of the house."

Goto: O⌈shoogatsu⌉ desu ne. Mu⌈kashi wa⌉ o⌈mochi o tsu⌉itari, to⌈kubetsu no ryo⌉ori o tsu⌈ku⌉ttari suru node, to⌈temo taihen de⌉shita. U⌈chi no na⌉ka mo so⌈oji shite okana⌉kereba na⌈ra⌉nai shi.
お正月ですね。昔はおもちをついたり、特別の料理を作ったりするので、とても大変でした。うちの中も掃除しておかなければならないし。

Kawa: A bit too long, isn't it. Let's break it. She starts with "It's the New Year," answering Mr. Smith's question.

Goto: O⌈shoogatsu⌉ desu ne.　お正月ですね。

Kawa: Next, "In the old days, we used to pound rice cakes, cook special dishes. So, there was a lot of work to do."

Goto: Mu⌈kashi wa⌉ o⌈mochi o tsu⌉itari, to⌈kubetsu no ryo⌉ori o tsu⌈ku⌉ttari suru node, to⌈temo taihen de⌉shita.
昔はおもちをついたり、特別の料理を作ったりするので、とても大変でした。

Kawa: I'm sure you've noticed this remark contains the second key sentence. **Mukashi wa** at the beginning means "in the old days." There's even more to do. She further carries on with, "We also had to clean up the inside of the house," which is based on the first key sentence.

Goto: U⌈chi no na⌉ka mo so⌈oji shite okana⌉kereba na⌈ra⌉nai shi.
うちの中も掃除しておかなければならないし。

Kawa: **Shi** at the end suggests that there's still something remaining unsaid. Mr. Smith wonders if it's not as busy as all that lately.

Goto: Ko⌈nogoro wa⌉ so⌈re hodo de⌉ mo ⌈na⌉i n desu ka.
このごろはそれほどでもないんですか。

Kawa: "But you don't have to do so much these days?" **Konogoro**, "these days;" **sore hodo de mo nai**, "not as much as." Yes, much easier nowadays. She says:

Goto: E⌉e, o⌈mochi mo⌉ sho⌈ogatu-yoo no ryo⌉ori mo mi⌈se⌉ de ka⌈ema⌉su kara ne.
ええ、おもちも正月用の料理も店で買えますからね。

Kawa: "No, not so busy these days, because we can buy rice cakes and special New Year dishes in the stores." **Shoogatsu-yoo no ryoori,**

"New Year dishes;" **kaemasu**, "we can buy." Now you'll listen to the whole conversation again.

◆ **Today's Conversation**

S: Oˡkusan no shigoto wa taˡihen deˡsu ne.
奥さんの仕事は大変ですね。

I: Eˡe, iˡsogashiˡi desu ˡneˡe. ええ、忙しいですねえ。

S: Iˡtsu ga iˡchibanˡ iˡsogashiˡi desu ka. いつが一番忙しいですか。

I: Oˡshoogatsuˡ desu ne. Muˡkashi waˡ oˡmochi o tsuˡitari, toˡkubetsu no ryoˡori o tsuˡkuˡttari suru node, toˡtemo taihen deˡshita. Uˡchi no naˡka mo soˡoji shite okanaˡkereba naˡraˡnai shi.
お正月ですね。昔はおもちをついたり、特別の料理を作ったりするので、とても大変でした。うちの中も掃除しておかなければならないし。

S: Koˡnogoro waˡ soˡre hodo deˡ mo ˡnaˡi n desu ka.
このごろはそれほどでもないんですか。

I: Eˡe, oˡmochi moˡ shoˡogatu-yoo no ryoˡori mo miˡseˡ de kaˡemaˡsu kara ne.
ええ、おもちも正月用の料理も店で買えますからね。

Kawa: You'll now review today's vocabulary. Please repeat aloud after Goto-san, who'll say each word or phrase twice. First, "New Year season."

Goto: Oˡshoogatsuˡ. お正月

Kawa: "Rice cake."

Goto: Oˡmochi. おもち

Kawa: "Special."

Goto: Toˡkubetsu no. 特別の

Kawa: "To clean."

Goto: Soˡoji shimaˡsu. 掃除します。

Kawa: Now, today's key sentences. This time, just listen to Goto-san. The first key sentence: "We have to clean up."

Goto: Soˡoji shite okanaˡkereba naˡrimaseˡn.
掃除しておかなければなりません。

Kawa: The second key sentence: "We used to pound rice cakes and cook special dishes, so there was a lot of work to do."

Goto: Oˡmochi o tsuˡitari, toˡkubetsu no ryoˡori o tsuˡkuˡttari suru node taˡihen deˡshita.
おもちをついたり、特別の料理を作ったりするので大変でした。

Kawa: Now before we wind up, let's listen to the whole dialogue again.

◆ **Today's Conversation**

S: Oˈkusan no shigoto wa taˈihen deˈsu ne.
奥さんの仕事は大変ですね。

I: Eˈe, iˈsogashiˈi desu ˈneˈe. ええ、忙しいですねえ。

S: Iˈtsu ga iˈchibanˈ iˈsogashiˈi desu ka. いつが一番忙しいですか。

I: Oˈshoogatsuˈ desu ne. Muˈkashi waˈ oˈmochi o tsuˈitari, toˈkubetsu no ryoˈori o tsuˈkuˈttari suru no de, toˈtemo taihen deˈshita. Uˈchi no naˈka mo soˈoji shite okanaˈkereba naˈraˈnai shi.
お正月ですね。昔はおもちをついたり、特別の料理を作ったりするので、とても大変でした。うちの中も掃除しておかなければならないし。

S: Koˈnogoro waˈ soˈre hodo deˈ mo ˈnaˈi n desu ka.
このごろはそれほどでもないんですか。

I: Eˈe, oˈmochi moˈ shoˈogatu-yoo no ryoˈori mo miˈseˈ de kaˈemaˈsu kara ne.
ええ、おもちも正月用の料理も店で買えますからね。

Notes

1. -tari…-tari suru ("to do such things as A and B")

This pattern is used to describe a state by giving some representative actions. We form the pattern by adding **-ri** to the informal past form of verbs. Usually two actions are given as examples to describe a state or condition, but sometimes only one action is given and other similar actions are only implied.

Kiˈnoˈo wa ˈnaˈni o shiˈmaˈshita ka. ("What did you do yesterday?")
Kaˈimono ni ittaˈri, toˈmodachi toˈ shoˈkuji o shitaˈri shimashita. ("I went shopping, had dinner with a friend, and so on.")
Teˈrebi o ˈmiˈtari shite imashita. ("I was doing things like watching TV.")
Kiˈyomizu-dera o miˈtari, Niˈjoˈo-joo i iˈttaˈri shimashita. ("I did such things as seeing Kiyomizu Temple and going to Nijo Castle, and so on.")

2. A mo B mo kaemasu. ("You can buy both A and B.")

If the verb is in the negative form, A **mo** B **mo** means "neither A nor B."

Taˈbako mo raˈitaa mo uˈtte imaˈsu. ("They sell both cigarettes and lighters.")
Suˈmisu-san mo Yaˈmada-san mo kimaseˈn deshita. ("Neither Mr. Smith nor Mr. Yamada came.")

Additional Vocabulary

juˈnbi	（準備）	preparation
meˈndoˈo na	（面倒な）	troublesome
riˈhatsuˈten	（理髪店）	barber shop

ka⌈mi⌉	(髪)	hair; hairdo
be⌈nkyo suru	(勉強する)	study
te⌈gami o ka⌉ku	(手紙を書く)	write letters
ji⌈sho o shi⌈rabe⌉ru	(辞書を調べる)	to check with dictionaries
e⌈ega o ⌈mi⌉ru	(映画を見る)	to see a movie
ryo⌉koo o suru	(旅行をする)	to travel
ta⌈noshi⌈i	(楽しい)	pleasant; fun
u⌈chi; i⌈e⌉	(家)	house; home
ji⌈nja	(神社)	Shinto shrines
ha⌈tsumo⌉ode	(初詣)	first visit of the year to a shrine or a temple

Exercises

1. Construct sentences with **-ta⌉ri...-ta⌉ri shi⌈ma⌉su** as shown in the example.

   Example: **i⌈ku; ku⌉ru→I⌈tta⌉ri, ki⌈ta⌉ri shimasu.**

   1. za⌈sshi o yo⌉mu; te⌈rebi o ⌈mi⌉ru
   2. ya⌈ma⌉ e i⌈ku; te⌈nisu o suru
   3. ryo⌉ori o tsukuru; so⌈oji o suru
   4. e⌈ega o ⌈mi⌉ru; to⌈modachi to⌉ ki⌈ssaten e iku
   5. be⌈nkyoo suru; te⌈gami o ka⌉ku

2. **-ta⌉ri...-ta⌉ri su⌈ru⌉ no de, ta⌈ihen de⌉shita.** Form sentences according to the example.

   Example: **o⌈mochi o tsu⌉ku; to⌈kubetsu no ryo⌉ori o tsu⌈ku⌉ru→O⌈mochi o tsu⌉itari, to⌈kubetsu no ryo⌉ori o tsu⌈ku⌉ttari suru node, ta⌈ihen de⌉shita.**

   1. so⌈oji o suru; ryo⌉ori o tsu⌉ku⌉ru
   2. shi⌈goto o suru; be⌈nkyoo o suru
   3. Ni⌈hongo o hana⌉su; ki⌈ku
   4. shi⌈nbun o yomu; za⌈sshi o shirabe⌉ru
   5. Ni⌈hongo ba⌉kari de ha⌈na⌉su; ka⌉ku

3. **-ta⌉ri...-ta⌉ri shite, to⌈temo tanoshi⌉katta desu.** Form sentences according to the example.

   Example: **e⌈ega o ⌈mi⌉ru; ki⌈ssa⌉ten ni ⌈ha⌉iru→E⌈ega o mitari, ki⌈ssa⌉ten ni ⌈ha⌉ittari shite, to⌈temo tanoshi⌉katta desu.**

   1. to⌈modachi to sake o no⌉mu; o⌈ishii ryo⌉ori o ta⌈be⌉ru
   2. e⌈ega o ⌈mi⌉ru; ka⌈raoke e iku
   3. ryo⌈koo o suru; to⌈modachi to a⌉u
   4. e⌉ o kaku; sha⌈shi o to⌉ru
   5. to⌈kubetsu no ryo⌉ori o ta⌈be⌉ru; ha⌈tsumo⌉ode ni iku
   6. o⌈sake o no⌉mu; ka⌈raoke ni iku
   7. ryo⌈koo no shashin o mi⌉ru; i⌈roiro⌉ ha⌈nashi⌉ o suru

4. -te o⌐kana⌐kereba narimasen.

Rewrite the following sentences according to the example.

Example: So⌐oji suru.→So⌐oji shite okana⌐kereba narimasen.

1. O⌐mochi o tsu⌐ku.
2. To⌐kubetsu no ryo⌐ori o tsu⌐ku⌐ru.
3. Bi⌐yo⌐oshitsu e iku.
4. Ri⌐hatsu⌐ten e iku.
5. Ka⌐mi⌐ o ⌐ki⌐ree ni suru.
6. Ki⌐mono o ju⌐nbi suru.
7. So⌐oji suru.
8. Sa⌐ke ya bi⌐iru o ka⌐u.
9. I⌐e no na⌐ka o ⌐ki⌐ree ni suru.
10. I⌐e no so⌐to o ⌐ki⌐ree ni suru.

5. Practice conversation using the sentences constructed in Exercise 4 above to create B's role.

Example: So⌐oji suru.→

A: O⌐shoogatsu no ma⌐e ni wa ⌐do⌐nna koto o shite oku no desu ka.
B: So⌐oji shite okana⌐kereba narimasen.
A: Ta⌐ihen de⌐su ne.

6. Now practice the dialogue using the cues given below and the -ta⌐ri…-ta⌐ri shite o⌐kana⌐kereba narimasen construction for B's role.

Example: so⌐oji suru; o⌐mochi o tsu⌐ku

A: O⌐shoogatsu no ma⌐e ni wa ⌐do⌐nna koto o shite oku no desu ka.
B: So⌐oji shita⌐ri, o⌐mochi o tsu⌐itari shite o⌐kana⌐kereba narimasen.
A: Ta⌐ihen de⌐su ne.

1. ryo⌐ri o tsu⌐ku⌐ru; so⌐oji suru
2. i⌐e no so⌐to o ⌐ki⌐ree ni suru; sa⌐ka ya bi⌐iru o ka⌐u
3. bi⌐yo⌐oshitsu e iku; ki⌐mono o ju⌐nbi suru
4. ri⌐hatsu⌐ten e iku; ha⌐na⌐ o ka⌐u
5. ka⌐mi⌐ o ⌐ki⌐ree ni suru; o⌐sake o kau

7. Are you able to understand the following dialogues?

1. A: I⌐tsu ga i⌐chiban isogashi⌐i desu ka.
   B: O⌐shoogatsu de⌐su ne. To⌐kubetsu no ryo⌐ori o tsu⌐ku⌐ttari, i⌐e no na⌐ka o so⌐oji shita⌐ri suru node to⌐temo taihan de⌐su.

2. A: I⌐tsu ga i⌐chiban isogashi⌐i desu ka.
   B: Ni⌐jihango⌐ro desu ne. Gi⌐nkoo e itta⌐ri, hi⌐to ga kita⌐ri shite to⌐temo isogashi⌐i desu.

3. A: Na⌐nyo⌐obi ga i⌐chiban tanoshi⌐i desu ka.

   B: Ni⌐chiyo⌐obi desu ne. A⌐sa o⌐soku⌐ made ne⌐te ita⌐ri, te⌐rebi o ⌐mi⌐tari, za⌐sshi o yo⌐ndari shite, yo⌐ku ya⌐sumema⌐su kara....

4. A: I⌐tsu ga i⌐chiban tanoshi⌐i desu ka.

   B: Do⌐yo⌐obi no ⌐go⌐go desu ne. E⌐ega o mitari, to⌐modachi to⌐ ki⌐ssa⌐ten ni i⌐tta⌐ri shite, ta⌐noshi⌐i desu.

8. Express the following dialogue in Japanese.

   A: You are having a party tonight, aren't you?

   B: Yes, I have to buy beer, clean the house, cook, etc.

   A: That's quite a bit of work. I stocked up on beer last night, so I'll bring some.

Answers

1. 1. Za⌐sshi o yo⌐ndari, ⌐te⌐rebi o ⌐mi⌐tari shimasu.
   2. Ya⌐ma⌐ e ittari, te⌐nisu o shi⌐ta⌐ri shimasu.
   3. Ryo⌐ori o tsu⌐ku⌐ttari, so⌐oji o shita⌐ri shimasu.
   4. E⌐ega o ⌐mi⌐tari, to⌐modachi to⌐ ki⌐ssa⌐ten e i⌐tta⌐ri shimasu.
   5. Be⌐nkyoo shita⌐ri, te⌐gami o ka⌐itari shimasu.

2. 1. So⌐oji o shita⌐ri, ⌐ryo⌐ori o tsu⌐ku⌐ttari suru node, ta⌐ihen de⌐shita.
   2. Shi⌐goto o shita⌐ri, be⌐nkyoo o shita⌐ri suru node ta⌐ihen de⌐shita.
   3. Ni⌐hongo o hana⌐shitari, ki⌐ita⌐ri suru node ta⌐ihen de⌐shita.
   4. Shi⌐nbun o yo⌐ndari, za⌐sshi o shira⌐betari suru node ta⌐ihen de⌐shita.
   5. Ni⌐hongo ba⌐kari de ha⌐na⌐shitari, ⌐ka⌐itari suru node ta⌐ihen de⌐shita.

3. 1. To⌐mogachi to⌐ sa⌐ke o no⌐ndari, o⌐ishii ryo⌐ori o ⌐ta⌐betari shite, to⌐temo tanoshi⌐katta desu.
   2. E⌐ega o mitari, ka⌐raoke e itta⌐ri shite, to⌐temo tanoshi⌐katta desu.
   3. Ryo⌐koo o shita⌐ri, to⌐modachi to a⌐ttari shite, to⌐temo tanoshi⌐katta desu.
   4. E⌐ o kaitari, sha⌐shin o to⌐ttari shite, to⌐temo tanoshi⌐katta desu.
   5. To⌐kubetsu no ryo⌐ori o ⌐ta⌐betari, ha⌐tsumo⌐ode ni i⌐tta⌐ri shite, to⌐temo tanoshi⌐katta desu.
   6. O⌐sake o no⌐ndari, ka⌐raoke ni itta⌐ri shite, to⌐temo tanoshi⌐katta desu.
   7. Ryo⌐koo no shashin o mi⌐tari i⌐roiro hanashi⌐ o shi⌐ta⌐ri shite to⌐temo tanoshi⌐katta desu.

4. 1. O⌐mochi o tu⌐ite okanakereba narimasen.
   2. To⌐kubetsu no ryo⌐ori o tsu⌐ku⌐tte okanakereba narimasen.
   3. Bi⌐yo⌐oshitsu e i⌐te okana⌐kereba narimasen.
   4. Ri⌐hatsu⌐ten e i⌐tte okana⌐kereba narimasen.
   5. Ka⌐mi⌐ o ⌐ki⌐ree ni shite okanakereba narimasen.
   6. Ki⌐mono o ju⌐nbi shite okanakereba narimasen.
   7. So⌐oji shite okana⌐kereba narimasen.
   8. Sa⌐ke ya bi⌐iru o ka⌐tte okana⌐kereba narimasen.
   9. I⌐e no na⌐ka o ⌐ki⌐ree ni shite okanakereba narimasen.
   10. I⌐e no so⌐to o ⌐ki⌐ree ni shite okanakereba narimasen.

6. 1. Ryo⌐ori o tsu⌐ku⌐ttari, so⌐oji shita⌐ri shite o⌐kana⌐kereba narimasen.
    2. I⌐e no so⌐to o ⌐ki⌐ree ni shitari, sa⌐ke ya bi⌐iru o ka⌐tta⌐ri shite o⌐kana⌐kereba narimasen.
    3. Bi⌐yo⌐oshitsu e ittari, ki⌐mono o ju⌐nbi shitari shite o⌐kana⌐kereba narimasen.
    4. Ri⌐hatsu⌐ten e i⌐tta⌐ri, ha⌐na⌐ o ka⌐tta⌐ri shite o⌐kana⌐kereba narimasen.
    5. Ka⌐mi⌐ o ⌐ki⌐ree ni shitari, o⌐sake o katta⌐ri shite o⌐kana⌐kereba narimasen.

7. 1. A: When is the busiest time for you?
       B: The New Year season. We make special dishes, clean the house, and so on, so we are very busy.

    2. A: When is the busiest time for you?
       B: Around 2:30. People come to visit, we go to the bank, etc. We are very busy.

    3. A: What day of the week is the happiest day for you?
       B: Sunday. I can rest well, doing such things as sleeping late in the morning, watching TV, and reading magazines, etc.

    4. A: When is the most delightful time for you?
       B: Saturday afternoon. Seeing a movie, going to a coffeeshop with my friends, etc., etc.— delightful!

8. A: Ko⌐nban ⌐pa⌐atii o su⌐ru⌐ n desu ne.
    B: E⌐e, bi⌐iru o ka⌐tta⌐ri, i⌐e⌐ o so⌐oji shita⌐ri, ryo⌐ori o tsu⌐ku⌐ttari shi⌐na⌐kereba naranai n desu.
    A: Ta⌐ihen de⌐su ne. Yu⌐ube bi⌐iru o ta⌐kusan katte okima⌐shita kara, mo⌐tte ikima⌐su yo.

LESSON
46

TE˥REBI NO KA˥BUKI CHUUKEE
BA˥NGUMI O MI˥NA˥GARA
テレビの歌舞伎中継番組を見ながら
Watching Kabuki on TV

Today's Conversation

Smith: **Ka˥buki no yakusha wa˥ mi˥nna˥ o˥toko˥ desu ka.**
歌舞伎の役者はみんな男ですか。
Are all kabuki players men?

Ito: **E˥e, so˥o desu.**
ええ、そうです。
Yes, they are.

Smith: **De˥mo, a˥rukikata˥ mo ha˥nashikata˥ mo ma˥rude˥ ˥onna no yo˥o desu ne.**
でも、歩き方も話し方もまるで女のようですね。
They look just like women, the way they walk and talk.

Ito: **So˥o desu ne.**
そうですね。
That's right.

Smith: **A˥no odori wa na˥ni ka ˥i˥mi ga ˥a˥ru n desu ka.**
あの踊りは何か意味があるんですか。
Does that dancing indicate anything?

Ito: **Ko˥ibito ga ni˥geta koto o ka˥nashiga˥tte i˥ru˥ n desu.**
恋人が逃げたことを悲しがっているんです。
It describes her sorrow over her lover deserting her.

Smith: **Na˥ze ˥ni˥geta n desu ka.**
なぜ逃げたんですか。

Why did he desert her?

Ito: **O'boosan de'su kara ke'kkon suru ko'to ga de'ki'nai n desu.**
お坊さんですから結婚することができないんです。
He can't marry because he is a priest.

TEREBI NO KABUKI CHUUKEE BANGUMI O MINAGARA
テレビの歌舞伎中継番組を見ながら
Watching Kabuki on TV

Kawa: Today, in Lesson 46, Mr. Smith enjoys a stage relay of kabuki on TV. He marvels at the incredible performance of kabuki actors playing the roles of women. Our first key sentence is, "They look just like women, the way they walk and talk."

Goto: **A'rukika'ta mo ha'nashika'ta mo o'nna no yo'o desu.**
歩き方も話し方も女のようです。

Kawa: **Arukikata** means "the way someone walks;" **hanashikata**, "the way someone talks;"…**no yoo desu**, "…is like someone" or "something."

Goto: **A'rukika'ta mo ha'nashika'ta mo o'nna no yo'o desu.**
歩き方も話し方も女のようです。

Kawa: Now, you'll change the part of something that's just like something else. "The voice," **koe**, and "the way they talk," **hanashikata**, which you've just learned. "They sound just like women, their voices and the way they talk."

Goto: **Ko'e mo ha'nashika'ta mo o'nna no yo'o desu.**
声も話し方も女のようです。

Kawa: As you have heard, you can use the same Japanese expression,… **onna no yoo desu** for "they sound just like women." What about their clothes and personal belongings? "They are just like women, what they wear and what they have around themselves."

Goto: **Ki'ru mono' mo mo'chimo'no mo o'nna no yo'o desu.**
着るものも持ちものも女のようです。

Kawa: Next, the second key sentence. Kabuki features many stylized dances, which are usually impassioned passages of kabuki. Mr. Smith is curious to know if the dance being performed in front of him has any meaning. Mrs. Ito explains to him, "She's grieving over her lover deserting her."

Goto: **Ko'ibito ga ni'geta koto o ka'nashiga'tte i'ru' n desu.**
恋人が逃げたことを悲しがっているんです。

Kawa: In this sentence, you didn't hear "she," did you? We don't use it here because the context is obvious enough in Japanese. **Koibito** means "lover." **Nigeta koto** literally means "the fact that her lover ran away," so in the context, "the fact that he deserted her," **kanashigatte iru n desu**, "is grieving over something." I hope you remember the emotionally emphasized **iru n desu**, "indeed she is." Let's say the second key sentence again: "She' grieving over her lover deserting her."

Goto: **Ko⌈ibito ga ni⌉geta koto o ka⌈nashiga⌉tte i⌈ru⌉ n desu.**
恋人が逃げたことを悲しがっているんです。

Kawa: Now, substitutions. "He is grieving over the failure in business." "The failure" itself is **shippai**; **shigoto**, "work" or "business."

Goto: **Shi⌈goto ni shippai shita koto⌉ o ka⌈nashiga⌉tte i⌈ru⌉ n desu.**
仕事に失敗したことを悲しがっているんです。

Kawa: "He's grieving over the failure in business," or "He is sad about the business failure." Let's try something else. "He is sad about the money he has lost." **Kane ga nakunatta koto** means "the fact that he has lost his money." "He's grieving over the money he has lost."

Goto: **Ka⌈ne ga nakunatta koto⌉ o ka⌈nashiga⌉tte i⌈ru⌉ n desu.**
金がなくなったことを悲しがっているんです。

♪ **Station Break** ▮▮▮▮▮▯▯▮▮▮

Kawa: Now, in the second half of this session, we'll discuss each dialogue. Listen to their conversation first.

◆ **Today's Conversation**

S: **Ka⌈buki no yakusha wa⌉ mi⌈nna⌉ o⌈toko⌉ desu ka.**
歌舞伎の役者はみんな男ですか。

I: **E⌉e, so⌉o desu.** ええ、そうです。

S: **De⌉mo, a⌈rukikata⌉ mo ha⌈nashikata⌉ mo ma⌈rude⌉ ⌈onna no yo⌉o desu ne.** でも、歩き方も話し方もまるで女のようですね。

I: **So⌉o desu ne.** そうですね。

S: **A⌈no odori wa na⌉ni ka ⌈i⌉mi ga ⌈a⌉ru n desu ka.**
あの踊りは何か意味があるんですか。

I: **Ko⌈ibito ga ni⌉geta koto o ka⌈nashiga⌉tte i⌈ru⌉ n desu.**
恋人が逃げたことを悲しがっているんです。

S: **Na⌉ze ⌈ni⌉geta n desu ka.** なぜ逃げたんですか。

I: **O⌈boosan de⌉su kara ke⌈kkon suru ko⌉to ga de⌈ki⌉nai n desu.**
お坊さんですから結婚することができないんです。

Kawa: Next, you'll listen to its English version.

◆ **Same Conversation in English**

S: Are all kabuki players men?

I: Yes, they are.

S: They look just like women, the way they walk and talk.

I: That's right.

S: Does that dancing indicate anything?

I: It describes her sorrow over her lover deserting her.

S: Why did he desert her?

I: He can't marry because he is a priest.

Kawa: Now each dialogue. We start with Mr. Smith's question: "Are all kubuki actors men?"

Goto: **Ka⌐buki no yakusha wa⌐ mi⌐nna⌐ o⌐toko⌐ desu ka.**
歌舞伎の役者はみんな男ですか。

Kawa: **Yakusha** means "actor." **Kabuki no yakusha,** "kabuki actor" or "actor<u>s</u>;" **minna,** "everyone." Now, listen again.

Goto: **Ka⌐buki no yakusha wa⌐ mi⌐nna⌐ o⌐toko⌐ desu ka.**
歌舞伎の役者はみんな男ですか。

Kawa: Answering that question, Mrs. Ito says, "Yes, they are."

Goto: **E⌐e, so⌐o desu.** ええ、そうです。

Kawa: This sentence literally means "Yes, that is so." Mr. Smith is much impressed with the incredible performance of the kabuki actors playing female roles. He comments, "They look just like women, the way they walk and talk."

Goto: **De⌐mo, a⌐rukika⌐ta mo ha⌐nashika⌐ta mo ma⌐rude onna no yo⌐o desu ne.** でも、歩き方も話し方もまるで女のようですね。 ───

Kawa: **Demo** is an informal "but." **Marude,** "just like." It's almost like the first key sentence, isn't it? We'll break it a little for more practice again. "The way they walk."

Goto: **A⌐rukika⌐ta.** 歩き方

Kawa: Next, "the way they talk."

Goto: **Ha⌐nashika⌐ta.** 話し方

Kawa: You can make "the way someone does" phrases such as "the way we read," **yomikata,** using this pattern. All you have to do here is just take out **-masu** from **yomimasu** and add **-kata,** "the way."

Goto: **Yo⌐mika⌐ta.** 読み方

Kawa: Next, try **kakimasu,** "to write," for "the way you write."

Goto: **Ka⌈kika⌉ta.** 書き方

Kawa: How about **tsukai-masu,** "to use," and "the way you use?"

Goto: **Tsu⌈kaikata.** 使い方

Kawa: Now, we get back to the dialogue. Mrs. Ito agrees, "Yes, that's right."

Goto: **So⌉o desu ne.** そうですね。

Kawa: Mr. Smith would like to know what the dance being played in front of him means. "Does that dance have some meaning?"

Goto: **A⌈no odori wa na⌉ni ka ⌈i⌉mi ga ⌈a⌉ru n desu ka.**
あの踊りは何か意味があるんですか。

Kawa: **Odori** means "dance;" **imi,** "meaning." **Nani ka imi ga aru n desu ka** means literally, "is there any meaning at all?"

Goto: **A⌈no odori wa na⌉ni ka ⌈i⌉mi ga ⌈a⌉ru n desu ka.**
あの踊りは何か意味があるんですか。

Kawa: Next, the second key sentence, spoken by Mrs. Ito: "Yes, she is grieving over her lover deserting her."

Goto: **Ko⌈ibito ga ni⌉geta koto o ka⌈nashiga⌉tte i⌈ru⌉ n desu.**
恋人が逃げたことを悲しがっているんです。

Kawa: Mr. Smith wonders, "Why did he desert her?"

Goto: **Na⌉ze ⌈ni⌉geta n desu ka.** なぜ逃げたんですか。

Kawa: **Nigeta,** "deserted." The emphatic **n desu ka** in **nigeta n desu ka** may be close to "why was he so heartless as to...." "Why was he so heartless as to desert her?"

Goto: **Na⌉ze ⌈ni⌉geta n desu ka.** なぜ逃げたんですか。

Kawa: Mrs. Ito's answer: "He can't marry her because he is a priest." "Marry," **kekkon suru,** and "can't marry," **kekkon suru koto ga dekinai.** Mind you, listeners, this can't be the case nowadays. You see, the story took place a few centuries ago during Japan's feudal times. Perhaps it's not unlike Catholic priests, who don't marry so long as they remain in the priesthood. "He can't marry her because he is a priest."

Goto: **O⌈boosan de⌉su kara ke⌈kkon suru ko⌉to ga de⌈ki⌉nai n desu.**
お坊さんですから結婚することができないんです。

Kawa: **Oboosan** means "priest." "Because he is a priest:"

Goto: **O⌈boosan de⌉su kara.** お坊さんですから

Kawa: "He can't marry her."

Goto: **Ke⌈kkon suru ko⌉to ga de⌈ki⌉nai n desu.**
結婚することができないんです。

Kawa: It's easier this time, isn't it? Let's now listen to the whole conversation again.

◆ **Today's Conversation**

S: **Ka⌈buki no yakusha wa⌉ mi⌈nna⌉ o⌈toko⌉ desu ka.**
　　歌舞伎の役者はみんな男ですか。

I: **E⌉e, so⌉o desu.** ええ、そうですね。

S: **De⌉mo, a⌈rukikata⌉ mo ha⌈nashikata⌉ mo ma⌈rude⌉ ⌈onna no yo⌉o desu ne.** でも、歩き方も話し方もまるで女のようですね。

I: **So⌉o desu ne.** そうですね。

S: **A⌈no odori wa na⌉ni ka ⌈i⌉mi ga ⌈a⌉ru n desu ka.**
　　あの踊りは何か意味があるんですか。

I: **Ko⌈ibito ga ni⌉geta koto o ka⌈nashiga⌉tte i⌈ru⌉ n desu.**
　　恋人が逃げたことを悲しがっているんです。

S: **Na⌉ze ⌈ni⌉geta n desu ka.** なぜ逃げたんですか。

I: **O⌈boosan de⌉su kara ke⌈kkon suru ko⌉to ga de⌈ki⌉nai n desu.**
　　お坊さんですから結婚することができないんです。

Kawa: Next, as usual, you'll practice today's vocabulary. Please repeat aloud after Goto-san, who will say each word or phrase twice. First, "dance."

Goto: **O⌈dori.** 踊り

Kawa: "Meaning."

Goto: **I⌉mi.** 意味

Kawa: "Priest."

Goto: **O⌈boosan.** お坊さん

Kawa: "Marry."

Goto: **Ke⌈kkon suru.** 結婚する。

Kawa: Now the key sentences again. This time, just listen to Goto-san. The first key sentence: "They look just like women, the way they walk and talk."

Goto: **A⌈rukika⌉ta mo ha⌈nashika⌉ta mo o⌈nna no yo⌉o desu.**
　　歩き方も話し方も女のようです。

Kawa: Next, the second key sentence. "She is grieving over her lover deserting her."

Goto: **Ko⌈ibito ga ni⌉geta koto o ka⌈nashiga⌉tte i⌈ru⌉ n desu.**
　　恋人が逃げたことを悲しがっているんです。

Kawa: Now, you've got one more chance to listen to their conversation again.

◆ **Today's Conversation**

S: **Ka⌈buki no yakusha wa⌉ mi⌈nna⌉ o⌈toko⌉ desu ka.**
　　歌舞伎の役者はみんな男ですか。

I:　E⌐e, so⌐o desu.　ええ、そうです。

S:　De⌐mo, a⌐rukikata⌐ mo ha⌐nashikata⌐ mo ma⌐rude⌐ ⌐onna no yo⌐o desu ne.　でも、歩き方も話し方もまるで女のようですね。

I:　So⌐o desu ne.　そうですね。

S:　A⌐no odori wa na⌐ni ka ⌐i⌐mi ga ⌐a⌐ru n desu ka.
あの踊りは何か意味があるんですか。

I:　Ko⌐ibito ga ni⌐geta koto o ka⌐nashiga⌐tte i⌐ru⌐ n desu.
恋人が逃げたことを悲しがっているんです。

S:　Na⌐ze ⌐ni⌐geta n desu ka.　なぜ逃げたんですか。

I:　O⌐boosan de⌐su kara ke⌐kkon suru ko⌐to ga de⌐ki⌐nai n desu.
お坊さんですから結婚することができないんです。

Notes

1. Ma⌐rude N no ⌐yo⌐o da. ("It looks as if it were N.")

N **no yoo da.** means "Something looks like (though it really is not) N." **Marude** emphasizes the "likeness."

2. arukikata ("the way someone walks")

-**masu** form stem verb plus -**kata** means "the way one does something." It also means "how to do…," as in **Ko⌐no denwa no⌐ tsu⌐kaikata ga wakarimase⌐n.** ("I don't know how to use this telephone.")

3. Ka⌐nashiga⌐tte iru. ("She's grieving.")

Adjective stem (i.e., the form with the final -**i** removed) plus -**garu** makes the adjective into a verb that can be used to describe the feelings and related actions of a third person. In describing such feeling-related actions, moreover, the -**te iru** pattern is used. In Japanese we cannot make a direct statement about others' feelings like **Ka⌐nashi⌐i desu.** This sentence means "I am sad." To express that someone else is sad, we can only say, "Someone is grieving." or "Someone appears to be sad."—**Ka⌐nashiga⌐tte imasu.** or **Ka⌐nashii yo⌐o desu.**

4. V -(r)u koto ga dekiru ("can do V")

　E⌐ego o hana⌐su koto ga de⌐kima⌐su. ("I can speak English.")
　Ha⌐yaku ⌐ka⌐eru koto wa de⌐kimase⌐n. ("I cannot go home early.")
　Ke⌐kkon suru koto⌐ ga de⌐kimase⌐n. ("I cannot get married.")

With -**suru** verbs, like **ke⌐kkon suru, ke⌐nsa suru,** or **be⌐nkyoo suru,** you can use **de⌐ki⌐ru** directly after the noun stem of the verb, as in **ke⌐kkon dekimase⌐n; ke⌐nsa dekimasu; be⌐nkyoo dekima⌐su.**

Additional Vocabulary

sa⌐bishi⌐i	(寂しい)	lonely
o⌐moshiro⌐i	(おもしろい)	interesting
X ga ho⌐shi⌐i.	(Xが欲しい)	I want X.
ka⌐nji	(漢字)	Chinese characters
ga⌐kusee	(学生)	students
se⌐nse⌐e	(先生)	teacher
wa⌐apuro	(ワープロ)	word processor
shi⌐ppai suru	(失敗する)	to fail
u⌐mareru	(生まれる)	to be born

Exercises

1. Substitute the cue words for the underlined words in the model sentence.

   Model Sentence: __O⌐toko⌐__ desu keredo, __o⌐nna__ no yo⌐o desu ne. ("They are men, but they are just like women, aren't they?")

   1. o⌐tona; ko⌐domo
   2. ko⌐domo; o⌐tona
   3. Ni⌐honji⌐n; ga⌐ikoku⌐jin
   4. ga⌐ikoku⌐jin; Ni⌐honji⌐n
   5. ga⌐kusee; se⌐nse⌐e
   6. o⌐nna⌐; o⌐toko⌐
   7. o⌐nna⌐ no ko; o⌐toko⌐ no ko
   8. ge⌐tsuyo⌐obi; ni⌐chiyo⌐obi
   9. to⌐modachi; ka⌐zoku
   10. o⌐ka⌐asan; o⌐ne⌐esan

2. Substitute as in Exercise 1.

   Model Sentence: __A⌐rukika⌐ta__ mo __ha⌐nashika⌐ta__ mo o⌐nna no yo⌐o desu.

   1. ka⌐o; ka⌐rada
   2. ko⌐e; ha⌐nashika⌐ta
   3. ki⌐ru mono⌐; mo⌐chimo⌐no
   4. ta⌐beka⌐ta; no⌐mika⌐ta

3. **So⌐re o [   ] -ga⌐tte iru n desu.**

   Use the appropriately modified form of the cue word to fill in the blank.

   Example: ka⌐nashi⌐i→So⌐re o kanashiga⌐tte iru n desu.

   1. o⌐moshiro⌐i
   2. u⌐reshi⌐i
   3. sa⌐bishi⌐i

4. ho⌐shi⌐i
5. ka⌐nashi⌐i

4. Use the word in the parentheses in the -ga⌐tte iru n desu pattern to complete each sentence.

Example: Ko⌐ibito ga ni⌐geta koto o (ka⌐nashi⌐i)→Ko⌐ibito ga ni⌐geta koto o ka⌐nashiga⌐tte iru n desu.

1. Tsu⌐uyaku no shigoto o (o⌐moshiro⌐i)
2. A⌐tarashi⌐i tomodachi ga ⌐de⌐kita koto o (u⌐reshi⌐i)
3. Go⌐shu⌐jin ga ga⌐ikoku e itte iru koto⌐ o (sa⌐bishi⌐i)
4. A⌐tara⌐shiku deta wa⌐apuro o (ho⌐shi⌐i)
5. Do⌐roboo ni haira⌐reta koto o (ka⌐nashi⌐i)

5. Substitute the cue for the underlined phrase in the model sentence.

Model Sentence: Ko⌐ibito ga iru koto⌐ o yo⌐roko⌐nde iru n desu.

1. ke⌐kkon de⌐kita
2. ko⌐domo ga umareta
3. shi⌐goto ga u⌐maku itta
4. ka⌐ne ga mooka⌐tta
5. i⌐i seehin ga ⌐de⌐kita

6. Following the example, construct B's response using either the ka⌐nashiga⌐tte iru n desu pattern or the yo⌐roko⌐nde iru n desu pattern, depending on the context.

Example: A: A⌐no⌐ hito, ko⌐ibito ga ni⌐geta n desu ka.
B: E⌐e, so⌐o desu. A⌐no⌐ hito wa, ko⌐ibito ga ni⌐geta koto o ka⌐nashiga⌐tte iru n desu.

1. A: A⌐no⌐ hito, shi⌐goto ni shippai shita⌐ n desu ka.
2. A: A⌐no⌐ hito, ko⌐domo ga umareta⌐ n desu ka.
3. A: A⌐no⌐ hito, shi⌐goto ga u⌐maku itte iru n desu ka.
4. A: A⌐no⌐ hito, ko⌐ibito ga ina⌐i n desu ka.
5. A: A⌐no⌐ hito, ki⌐ppu ga kaeta⌐ n desu ka.

7. Tell your friend in Japanese:

1. that Mr. Tanaka is just like an American in the way he talks and the way he does his work.
2. that your mother is happy because she is going to Italy in June.
3. that that person is sad because she has no children.
4. that that man is sad because he cannot marry his girlfriend.
5. that you don't know how to read this kanji.

8. From the list given below, choose the appropriate ending or response for the following sentences.

1. A⌐no⌐ ko wa ⌐ma⌐da ⌐ju⌐ugosai desu ga,
2. Da⌐igaku ni ha⌐ireta node,
3. O⌐okikute ⌐u⌐mi no yoo desu ga,
4. A⌐no⌐ ko wa o⌐to⌐osan ni ⌐yo⌐ku ni⌐te ima⌐su ne.
5. Na⌐ze ke⌐kkon deki⌐nai n desu ka.
6. Te⌐nki ga ⌐i⌐i hi wa.

a) O⌐boosan da⌐ kara desu.
b) u⌐reshiga⌐tte imasu yo.
c) Ha⌐nashika⌐ta mo a⌐rukika⌐ta mo o⌐naji de⌐su ne.
d) ma⌐ru de⌐ o⌐tona no yo⌐o desu.
e) Fu⌐ji-san o ⌐mi⌐ru koto ga dekimasu.
f) ka⌐wa⌐ desu.

Answers ———————————————————————————————

1. 1. O⌐tona de⌐su keredo, ko⌐domo no yo⌐o desu ne.
   2. Ko⌐domo de⌐su keredo, o⌐tona no yo⌐o desu ne.
   3. Ni⌐honji⌐n desu keredo, ga⌐ikoku⌐jin no yoo desu ne.
   4. Ga⌐ikoku⌐jin desu keredo, Ni⌐hon-ji⌐n no yoo desu ne.
   5. Ga⌐kusee de⌐su keredo, se⌐nse⌐e no yoo desu ne.
   6. O⌐nna⌐ desu keredo, o⌐toko no yo⌐o desu ne.
   7. O⌐nna⌐ no ko desu keredo, o⌐toko⌐ no ko no yoo desu ne.
   8. Ge⌐tsuyo⌐obi desu keredo, ni⌐chiyo⌐obi no yoo desu ne.
   9. To⌐modachi de⌐su keredo, ka⌐zoku no yoo desu ne.
   10. O⌐ka⌐asan desu keredo, o⌐ne⌐esan no yoo desu ne.

2. 1. Ka⌐o mo⌐ ka⌐rada mo⌐ o⌐nna no yo⌐o desu.
   2. Ko⌐e mo ha⌐nashika⌐ta mo o⌐nna no yo⌐o desu.
   3. Ki⌐ru mono⌐ mo mo⌐chimo⌐no mo o⌐nna no yo⌐o desu.
   4. Ta⌐beka⌐ta mo no⌐mika⌐ta mo o⌐nna no yo⌐o desu.

3. 1. So⌐re o omoshiroga⌐tte iru n desu.
   2. So⌐re o ureshiga⌐tte iru n desu.
   3. So⌐re o sabishiga⌐tte iru n desu.
   4. So⌐re o hoshiga⌐tte iru n desu.
   5. So⌐re o kanashiga⌐tte iru n desu.

4. 1. Tsu⌐uyaku no shigoto o o⌐moshiroga⌐tte iru n desu.
   2. A⌐tarashi⌐i tomodachi ga ⌐de⌐kita koto o u⌐reshiga⌐tte iru n desu.
   3. Go⌐shu⌐jin ga ga⌐ikoku e itte iru koto⌐ o sa⌐bishiga⌐tte iru n desu.
   4. A⌐tarashi⌐ku ⌐de⌐ta wa⌐apuro o hoshiga⌐tte iru n desu.
   5. Do⌐roboo ni haira⌐reta koto o ka⌐nashiga⌐tte iru n desu.

5. 1. Ke⌐kkon de⌐kita koto o yo⌐roko⌐nde iru n desu.
   2. Ko⌐domo ga umareta koto⌐ o yo⌐roko⌐nde iru n desu.
   3. Shi⌐goto ga u⌐maku itta koto o yo⌐roko⌐nde iru n desu.

    4. Ka⌐ne ga mooka⌐tta koto o yo⌐roko⌐nde iru n desu.

    5. I⌐i seehin ga ⌐de⌐kita koto o yo⌐roko⌐nde iru n desu.

6. 1. E⌐e, so⌐o desu. Shi⌐goto ni shippai shita koto⌐ o ka⌐nashiga⌐tte iru n desu.

    2. E⌐e, so⌐o desu. Ko⌐domo ga umareta koto⌐ o yo⌐roko⌐nde iru n desu.

    3. E⌐e, so⌐o desu. Shi⌐goto ga u⌐maku itte iru koto⌐ o yo⌐roko⌐nde iru n desu.

    4. E⌐e, so⌐o desu. Ko⌐ibito ga inai koto⌐ o ka⌐nashiga⌐tte iru n desu.

    5. E⌐e, so⌐o desu. Ki⌐ppu ga kaeta koto⌐ o yo⌐roko⌐nde iru n desu.

7. 1. Ta⌐naka-san wa⌐ ha⌐nashika⌐ta mo shi⌐goto no shikata mo⌐ A⌐merika⌐jin no yoo desu ne.

    2. Ha⌐ha wa ro⌐kugatu⌐ ni I⌐tariya e iku koto⌐ o u⌐reshiga⌐tte imasu.

    3. A⌐no⌐ hito wa ko⌐domo ga inai koto⌐ o ka⌐nashiga⌐tte imasu.

    4. A⌐no otoko no hito⌐ wa ko⌐ibito to kekkon deki⌐nai koto o ka⌐nashiga⌐tte imasu.

    5. Ko⌐no kanji no yomika⌐ta ga wa⌐karimse⌐n.

8. 1. (d)

    2. (b)

    3 (f)

    4. (c)

    5. (a)

    6. (e)

LESSON
47

TE˥REBI NO SU˥MOO O MINA˥GARA
テレビの相撲を見ながら
Watching Sumo on TV

	Today's Conversation

Smith: **Mo˥o o˹watta˥ n desu ka.**
もう終わったんですか。
Is it over already?

Ito: **E˥e, hi˹to˥ri ga a˹ite˥ o do˹hyoo no so˥to e o˹shida˥shita n desu.**
ええ、ひとりが相手を土俵の外へ押しだしたんです。
Yes. The wrestler pushed his opponent out of the ring.

Smith: **Su˹moo no shiai tte zu˹ibun ji˹kan ga mijika˥i n desu ne.**
相撲の試合ってずいぶん時間が短いんですね。
Sumo matches are very short, aren't they?

Ito: **So˥o desu ne.**
そうですね。
That's right.

Smith: **A˹nna ni futo˥tte iru no ni, zu˥ibun ˹ha˥yaku u˹goki-ma˥su ne.**
あんなに太っているのに、ずいぶん早く動きますね。
The wrestlers move very quickly even though they are so heavy.

Ito: **E˥e, ma˥inichi ki˹bishi˥i re˹nshuu o shite iru˥ node,**

ka⌐rada ga yo⌐ku u⌐go⌐ku n desu ne.
ええ、毎日きびしい練習をしているので体がよく動くんですね。
Yes. They train very hard every day, so they can move quickly.

TEREBI NO SUMOO O MINAGARA
テレビの相撲を見ながら
Watching Sumo on TV

Kawa:　Today, in Lesson 47, Mr. Smith watches sumo matches on TV at the Itos'. Sumo is Japan's traditional wrestling, which is very popular in this country. He's surprised to see that heavy sumo wrestlers are moving so quickly on the ring. He comments, "Even though they're fat, their bodies move pretty quickly, don't they?"

Goto:　**Fu⌐to⌐tte i⌐ru⌐ no ni ka⌐rada ga yo⌐ku u⌐gokima⌐su ne.**
太っているのに体がよく動きますね。

Kawa:　This is our first key sentence. **Futotte iru** means "to be fat;" **no ni**, "even though;" **yoku**, "well," but in this case it actually means "pretty quickly;" **karada**, "body" or "bodies;" **ugokimasu**, "to move." Once again please.

Goto:　**Fu⌐to⌐tte i⌐ru⌐ no ni ka⌐rada ga yo⌐ku u⌐gokima⌐su ne.**
太っているのに体がよく動きますね。

Kawa:　Now, a few substitutions. "Even though they're tired, their bodies move pretty quickly, don't they?" "Even though they're tired" is **tsukarete iru no ni.**

Goto:　**Tsu⌐ka⌐rete i⌐ru⌐ no ni ka⌐rada ga yo⌐ku u⌐gokima⌐su ne.**
疲れているのに体がよく動きますね。

Kawa:　How about "Even though they're hungry, their bodies move pretty quickly, don't they?" "Even though they're hungry," **onaka ga suite iru no ni. Onaka ga suite iru** means literally "the stomach is empty."

Goto:　**O⌐naka ga suite iru⌐ no ni ka⌐rada ga yo⌐ku u⌐gokima⌐su ne.**
おなかがすいているのに体がよく動きますね。

Kawa:　One more. "Even though they're old, their bodies move pretty quickly." "Old" in this case is **toshi o totte iru.**

Goto:　**To⌐shi⌐ o totte iru no ni ka⌐rada ga yo⌐ku u⌐gokima⌐su ne.**
年をとっているのに体がよく動きますね。

Kawa:　The second key sentence is, "They train very hard every day, so their bodies move around quickly." "Every day," **mainichi**; "hard," **kibishii**; "training," **renshuu**.

Goto: **Ma⌐inichi ki⌐bishi⌐i re⌐nshuu o shite iru⌐ node ka⌐rada ga yo⌐ku u⌐go⌐ku n desu ne.**
毎日きびしい練習をしているので体がよく動くんですね。

Kawa: **Shite iru** means "is doing." "They train very hard everyday, so…." Listen.

Goto: **Ma⌐inichi ki⌐bishi⌐i re⌐nshuu o shite iru⌐ node.**
毎日きびしい練習をしているので、

Kawa: The key word is **node**, "because" or "as." "Their bodies move around quickly, don't they?"

Goto: **Ka⌐rada ga yo⌐ku u⌐go⌐ku n desu ne.**　体がよく動くんですね。

Kawa: Now the whole sentence. "They train very hard every day, so their bodies move around quickly."

Goto: **Ma⌐inichi ki⌐bishi⌐i re⌐nshuu o shite iru⌐ node ka⌐rada ga yo⌐ku u⌐go⌐ku n desu ne.**
毎日きびしい練習をしているので体がよく動くんですね。

Kawa: Let's now change the second half. "They train very hard every day, so they can swim well." "Can swim," **oyogeru**.

Goto: **Ma⌐inichi ki⌐bishi⌐i re⌐nshuu o shite iru⌐ node ⌐yo⌐ku o⌐yoge⌐ru n desu ne.**　毎日きびしい練習をしているのでよく泳げるんですね。

Kawa: Next, "speaking." "They train very hard every day, so they can speak well." "Can speak well," **yoku hanaseru**.

Goto: **Ma⌐inichi ki⌐bishi⌐i re⌐nshuu o shite iru⌐ node ⌐yo⌐ku ha⌐nase⌐ru n desu ne.**　毎日きびしい練習をしているのでよく話せるんですね。

Kawa: Then, "reading." "They train very hard everyday, so they can read well." "Can read well," **yoku yomeru**.

Goto: **Ma⌐inichi ki⌐bishi⌐i re⌐nshuu o shite iru⌐ node ⌐yo⌐ku yo⌐me⌐ru n desu ne.**　毎日きびしい練習をしているのでよく読めるんですね。

♪ **Station Break** ꜱꜱꜱꜱꜱꜱꜱꜱꜱꜱꜱꜱꜱꜱꜱꜱꜱꜱꜱꜱꜱꜱꜱꜱ

Kawa: In the second half of this program, we'll discuss each dialogue as usual. Listen to the whole conversation first.

◆ **Today's Conversation**

S: **Mo⌐o o⌐watta⌐ n desu ka.**　もう終わったんですか。

I: **E⌐e, hi⌐to⌐ri ga a⌐ite⌐ o do⌐hyoo no so⌐to e o⌐shida⌐shita n desu.**
ええ、ひとりが相手を土俵の外へ押しだしたんです。

S: **Su⌐moo no shiai tte zu⌐ibun ji⌐kan ga mijika⌐i n desu ne.**
相撲の試合ってずいぶん時間が短いんですね。

I: **So⌐o desu ne.** そうですね。

S: **A⌐nna ni futo⌐tte iru no ni, zu⌐ibun ⌐ha⌐yaku u⌐gokima⌐su ne.**
あんなに太っているのに、ずいぶん早く動きますね。

I: **E⌐e, ma⌐inichi ki⌐bishi⌐i re⌐nshuu o shite iru⌐ node, ka⌐rada ga yo⌐ku u⌐go⌐ku n desu ne.**
ええ、毎日きびしい練習をしているので体がよく動くんですね。

Kawa: Next, you'll listen to its English version.

◆ Same Conversation in English

S: Is it over already?

I: Yes. The wrestler pushed his opponent out of the ring.

S: Sumo matches are very short, aren't they?

I: That's right.

S: The wrestlers move very quickly even though they are so heavy.

I: Yes. They train very hard every day, so they can move quickly.

Kawa: Now we study each dialogue one by one. Watching the sumo matches, Mr. Smith was a bit amazed because nearly every match came to an end so quickly. "Is it over already?" Mr. Smith remarks. "Be over" is **owatta** in this context. Listen to Goto-san again.

Goto: **Mo⌐o o⌐watta⌐ n desu ka.** もう終わったんですか。

Kawa: Mr. Ito explains to him that it's over now because one of the wrestlers pushed his opponent out of the ring. "One of them" is **hitori,** in this case. "Push out," **oshidasu.** "Opponent" is **aite;** "sumo ring" is **dohyoo.**

Goto: **E⌐e, hi⌐to⌐ri ga a⌐ite⌐ o do⌐hyoo no so⌐to e o⌐shida⌐shita n desu.**
ええ、ひとりが相手を土俵の外へ押しだしたんです。

Kawa: "Yes. One of them pushed his opponent out of the ring." Listen again.

Goto: **E⌐e, hi⌐to⌐ri ga a⌐ite⌐ o do⌐hyoo no so⌐to e o⌐shida⌐shita n desu.**
ええ、ひとりが相手を土俵の外へ押しだしたんです。

Kawa: Mr. Smith's honest impression is that sumo matches are very short.

Goto: **Su⌐moo no shiai tte zu⌐ibun ji⌐kan ga mijika⌐i n desu ne.**
相撲の試合ってずいぶん時間が短いんですね。

Kawa: "Sumo matches are very short, aren't they?" **Sumo no shiai tte** is often used colloquially with emotional emphasis. The neutral expression would be:

Goto: **Su⌐moo no shiai wa.** 相撲の試合は

Kawa: "Sumo matches are...."

Goto: **Zu⌐ibun ji⌐kan ga mijika⌐i n desu ne.**
ずいぶん時間が短いんですね。

Kawa: **Zuibun**, "very" or, sometimes, "very much;" **jikan ga mijikai**, "time is short." Now put them together: "Sumo matches are very short, aren't they?"

Goto: **Su⌈moo no shiai tte zu⌉ibun ji⌈kan ga mijika⌉i n desu ne.**
相撲の試合ってずいぶん時間が短いんですね。

Kawa: Mr. Ito simply agrees, saying, "That's right."

Goto: **So⌉o desu ne.** そうですね。

Kawa: Next, you'll hear an expression that'll remind you of the first key sentence. "Even though they are so fat, the wrestlers move pretty quickly."

Goto: **A⌈nna ni futo⌉tte iru no ni, zu⌉ibun ⌈ha⌉yaku u⌈gokima⌉su ne.**
あんなに太っているのに、ずいぶん早く動きますね。

Kawa: **Anna ni** means "so much." "The wrestlers move pretty quickly."

Goto: **Zu⌉ibun ⌈ha⌉yaku u⌈gokima⌉su ne.** ずいぶん早く動きますね。

Kawa: "The wrestlers" in the sentence was not mentioned as being obvious. Let's listen to the whole sentence this time.

Goto: **A⌈nna ni futo⌉tte iru no ni, zu⌉ibun ⌈ha⌉yaku u⌈gokima⌉su ne.**
あんなに太っているのに、ずいぶん早く動きますね。

Kawa: Mr. Ito explains the reason why they can move so quickly. "Yes. They train very hard every day, so their bodies move around quickly."

Goto: **E⌉e, ma⌉inichi ki⌈bishi⌉i re⌈nshuu o shite iru⌉ node, ka⌈rada ga yo⌉ku u⌈go⌉ku n desu ne.**
ええ、毎日きびしい練習をしているので体がよく動くんですね。

Kawa: **Ee** is an informal "yes." Let's deal with each part of the sentence slightly in a literal manner. "As they are doing hard practice every day."

Goto: **Ma⌉inichi ki⌈bishi⌉i re⌈nshuu o shite iru⌉ node.**
毎日きびしい練習をしているので

Kawa: "Their bodies move around quickly, don't they?"

Goto: **Ka⌈rada ga yo⌉ku u⌈go⌉ku n desu ne.** 体がよく動くんですね。

Kawa: Now you'll listen to the whole conversation again.

◆ **Today's Conversation**

S: **Mo⌉o o⌈watta⌉ n desu ka.** もう終わったんですか。

I: **E⌉e, hi⌈to⌉ri ga a⌈ite⌉ o do⌈hyoo no so⌉to e o⌈shida⌉shita n desu.**
ええ、ひとりが相手を土俵の外へ押しだしたんです。

S: **Su⌈moo no shiai tte zu⌉ibun ji⌈kan ga mijika⌉i n desu ne.**
相撲の試合ってずいぶん時間が短いんですね。

I: **So⌉o desu ne.** そうですね。

S: **A⌈nna ni futo⌉tte iru no ni, zu⌉ibun ⌈ha⌉yaku u⌈gokima⌉su ne.**
あんなに太っているのに、ずいぶん早く動きますね。

I:　E⌐e, ma⌐inichi ki⌐bishi⌐i re⌐nshuu o shite iru⌐ node, ka⌐rada ga yo⌐ku u⌐go⌐ku n desu ne.
　　ええ、毎日きびしい練習をしているので体がよく動くんですね。

Kawa:　You'll now review today's vocabulary. Please repeat aloud after Goto-san, who'll say each word or phrase twice. First, "opponent."

Goto:　A⌐ite⌐. 相手

Kawa:　"Match" or "matches."

Goto:　Shi⌐ai. 試合

Kawa:　"Body" or "bodies."

Goto:　Ka⌐rada. 体

Kawa:　"Short."

Goto:　Mi⌐jika⌐i. 短い

Kawa:　Now, today's key sentences. This time, just listen to Goto-san. Today's first key sentence: "Even though they're fat, the wrestlers move pretty quickly."

Goto:　Fu⌐to⌐tte i⌐ru⌐ no ni ka⌐rada ga yo⌐ku u⌐gokima⌐su ne.
　　太っているのに体がよく動きますね。

Kawa:　The second key sentence: "They train very hard everyday, so their bodies move around quickly."

Goto:　Ma⌐inichi ki⌐bishi⌐i re⌐nshuu o shite iru⌐ node ka⌐rada ga yo⌐ku u⌐go⌐ku n desu ne.
　　毎日きびしい練習をしているので体がよく動くんですね。

Kawa:　Now, before we wind up, let's listen to the whole dialogue again.

◆ Today's Conversation

S:　Mo⌐o o⌐watta⌐ n desu ka. もう終わったんですか。

I:　E⌐e, hi⌐to⌐ri ga a⌐ite⌐ o do⌐hyoo no so⌐to e o⌐shida⌐shita n desu.
　　ええ、ひとりが相手を土俵の外へ押しだしたんです。

S:　Su⌐moo no shiai tte zu⌐ibun ji⌐kan ga mijika⌐i n desu ne.
　　相撲の試合ってずいぶん時間が短いんですね。

I:　So⌐o desu ne. そうですね。

S:　A⌐nna ni futo⌐tte iru no ni, zu⌐ibun ⌐ha⌐yaku u⌐gokima⌐su ne.
　　あんなに太っているのに、ずいぶん早く動きますね。

I:　E⌐e, ma⌐inichi ki⌐bishi⌐i re⌐nshuu o shite iru⌐ node, ka⌐rada ga yo⌐ku u⌐go⌐ku n desu ne.
　　ええ、毎日きびしい練習をしているので体がよく動くんですね。

Notes

1. Hi⌐to⌐ri ga a⌐ite⌐ o o⌐shida⌐shita. ("One wrestler pushed his opponent out.")

Here **a⌐ite⌐** means "opponent." The word **a⌐ite⌐**, however, also means other things. Basically, it indicates someone or some party that does something with you together "face-to-face" or, sometimes, "hand-in-hand." Here are some examples:

te⌐nisu no aite	("one you play tennis with")
ke⌐kkon a⌐ite	("marriage partner")
ha⌐nashi a⌐ite	("the person you talk to or with")
a⌐sobi a⌐ite	("playmate")

2. X tte

This form, meaning "as for what you call X..." is used only in rather informal conversation and adds emotional emphasis. **Tte** is not used in neutral, declarative sentences or in writing; **wa** is used instead.

> **Ya⌐mada-san tte⌐ o⌐moshiro⌐i hito desu ne.**
> **To⌐kyoo tte⌐ ku⌐ruma mo hito mo o⌐oi tokoro desu ne.**
> **Ko⌐no hen tte be⌐nri desu yo.**

Additional Vocabulary

o⌐sumoo-san	（お相撲さん）	sumo wrestlers (familiar term; the formal term is **rikishi**)
ya⌐sete iru	（やせている）	thin, skinny
se⌐ ga ta⌐ka⌐i	（背が高い）	tall
se⌐ ga hi⌐ku⌐i	（背が低い）	short
ka⌐tsu	（勝つ）	to win
ma⌐keru	（負ける）	to lose
(su⌐moo o) to⌐ru	（相撲をとる）	to wrestle
ya⌐waraka⌐i	（やわらかい）	soft; flexible
ka⌐tai	（かたい）	hard; rigid
ha⌐shi⌐ru	（走る）	to run
o⌐yo⌐gu	（泳ぐ）	to swim

Exercises

1. Substitute the cue for the underlined phrase in the model sentence.

   Model Sentence: **Fu⌐to⌐tte iru** no ni, ka⌐rada ga yo⌐ku u⌐gokima⌐su ne.

   1. **tsu⌐ka⌐rete iru**
   2. **a⌐mari renshuu shina⌐i**
   3. **to⌐shi⌐ o ⌐to⌐tte iru**
   4. **o⌐naka ga suite iru**
   5. **ki⌐no⌐o made byo⌐oki da⌐tta**
   6. **a⌐shi⌐ ga i⌐ta⌐i**

2. Change the cue to the formal form and substitute it for the underlined phrase in the model sentence.

Model Sentence: de⌈ki⌉nakatta→Zu⌈ibun re⌈nshuu shita⌉ no ni, <u>de⌈kimase⌉n deshita</u>.

1. ka⌈te⌉nakatta
2. ma⌈keta
3. wa⌈kara⌉nakatta
4. yo⌈me⌉nakatta
5. ka⌈ke⌉nakatta

3. Substituting the cue words from Exercise 2 (making necessary changes) for the underlined portions, practice the following dialogue.

A: <u>De⌈kimase⌉n deshita</u>.
B: Re⌈nshuu shina⌉katta n desu ka.
A: I⌈ie, zu⌈ibun re⌈nshuu shita⌉ n desu ga, <u>de⌈kimase⌉n deshita</u>.
B: So⌈re wa zanne⌉n deshita ⌈ne⌉e. ("That's too bad!")

4. Substitute the cue for the underlined word in the model sentence.

Model Sentence: <u>Wa⌈ka⌉i</u> no ni be⌈nkyoo o shina⌉i no wa i⌈kemase⌉n ne.

1. ji⌈kan ga a⌉ru
2. a⌈tama⌉ ga ⌈i⌉i
3. ge⌉nki da (Hint: **da** or **de⌉su** changes to **na** before **no**.)
4. ga⌈kusee da
5. a⌈shita te⌉suto ga ⌈a⌉ru

5. Substitute the cue for the underlined phrase in the model sentence.

Model Sentence: Ma⌉inichi ki⌈bishi⌉i re⌈nshuu o shite iru⌉ node, <u>ka⌈rada ga yo⌉ku u⌈go⌉ku</u> n desu ne.

1. ha⌉yaku ha⌈shire⌉ru
2. shi⌈ai ni ka⌉teta
3. yo⌉ku yo⌈me⌉ru
4. yo⌉ku ha⌈nase⌉ru
5. yo⌉ku o⌈yoge⌉ru
6. ki⌉ree na ⌈ko⌉e ga ⌈de⌉ru

6. Substituting the cues from Exercise 5 for the underlined portions (and making necessary changes), practice the following dialogue.

A: A⌈nna ni⌉ to⌈shi⌉ o ⌈to⌉tte iru no ni, <u>ka⌈rada ga yo⌉ku u⌈gokima⌉su</u> ne.

B: E⌐e, ma⌐inichi ki⌐bishi⌐i re⌐nshuu o shite iru⌐ node, <u>ka⌐rada ga yo⌐ku u⌐go⌐ku</u> n desu ne.

A: Ta⌐ishita mo⌐no⌐ desu ne. ("That's really great!")

7. Complete or respond to the following sentences using phrases from the list given below.

1. A⌐no⌐ hito wa ⌐i⌐tsumo ⌐zu⌐ibun ta⌐kusan tabe⌐ru no ni
2. Ma⌐inichi ha⌐shi⌐ru re⌐nshuu o shite iru⌐ node
3. To⌐shi⌐ o ⌐to⌐tte iru node
4. Su⌐moo no shiai wa
5. Ma⌐da ke⌐kkon shina⌐i n desu ka.
6. A⌐rashiyama tte
7. Shi⌐nka⌐nsen wa hi⌐ko⌐oki
8. Ga⌐kusee na⌐ no ni
9. A⌐no osumoo-san wa⌐ fu⌐to⌐tte iru no ni
10. Do⌐hyoo no so⌐to e o⌐shidasare⌐reba

a) zu⌐ibun ji⌐kan ga mijika⌐i desu.
b) be⌐nkyoo ba⌐kari shite imasu.
c) fu⌐to⌐tte imasu ne.
d) ha⌐yaku ha⌐shiremase⌐n.
e) yo⌐ri wa o⌐so⌐i desu kedo….
f) ya⌐sete ima⌐su ne.
g) zu⌐ibun ⌐ha⌐yaku u⌐gokima⌐su ne.
h) sa⌐kura no meesho⌐ da soo desu ne.
i) ma⌐kema⌐su.
j) zu⌐ibun ⌐ha⌐yaku ha⌐shire⌐ru yoo ni na⌐rima⌐shita.
k) be⌐nkyoo shimase⌐n.
l) Shi⌐ta⌐i n desu ga, i⌐i aite ga i⌐na⌐i n desu yo.
m) ka⌐chima⌐su
n) yo⌐ri ha⌐ya⌐i desu kedo….

Answers ————————————————

1. 1. Tsu⌐ka⌐rete iru no ni, ka⌐rada ga yo⌐ku u⌐gokima⌐su ne.
   2. A⌐mari renshuu shina⌐i no ni, ka⌐rada ga yo⌐ku u⌐gokima⌐su ne.
   3. To⌐shi⌐ o ⌐to⌐tte iru no ni, ka⌐rada ga yo⌐ku u⌐gokima⌐su ne.
   4. O⌐naka ga suite iru⌐ no ni, ka⌐rada ga yo⌐ku u⌐gokima⌐su ne.
   5. Ki⌐no⌐o made byo⌐oki da⌐tta no ni, ka⌐rada ga yo⌐ku u⌐gokima⌐su ne.
   6. A⌐shi⌐ ga i⌐ta⌐i no ni, ka⌐rada ga yo⌐ku u⌐gokima⌐su ne.

2. 1. Zu⌐ibun re⌐nshuu shita⌐ no ni, ka⌐temase⌐n deshita.
   2. Zu⌐ibun re⌐nshuu shita⌐ no ni, ma⌐kema⌐shita.
   3. Zu⌐ibun re⌐nshuu shita⌐ no ni, wa⌐karimase⌐n deshita.
   4. Zu⌐ibun re⌐nshuu shita⌐ no ni, yo⌐memase⌐n deshita.
   5. Zu⌐ibun re⌐nshuu shita⌐ no ni, ka⌐kemase⌐n deshita.

4. 1. Jiˈkan ga aˈru no ni, beˈnkyoo o shinaˈi no wa iˈkemaseˈn ne.
   2. Aˈtamaˈ ga ˈiˈi no ni, beˈnkyoo o shinaˈi no wa iˈkemaseˈn ne.
   3. Geˈnki na no ni, beˈnkyoo o shinaˈi no wa iˈkemaseˈn ne.
   4. Gaˈkusee naˈ no ni, beˈnkyoo o shinaˈi no wa iˈkemaseˈn ne.
   5. Aˈshita teˈsuto ga ˈaˈru no ni, beˈnkyoo o shinaˈi no wa iˈkemaseˈn ne.

7. 1 (f)
   2. (j)
   3. (d)
   4. (a)
   5. (l)
   6. (h)
   7. (e)
   8. (k)
   9. (g)
   10. (i)

TEˈREBI NO RYOˈORI BAˈNGUMI O MIˈNAˈGARA
テレビの料理番組を見ながら
Watching a Cooking Program on TV

Today's Conversation

Smith: **Niˈhon-ryoˈori to itte mo, zaˈiryoˈo wa yuˈnyuuhin ga oˈoi soo desu ne.**

日本料理といっても、材料は輸入品が多いそうですね。

Although it's called Japanese cuisine, most of the raw materials are imported, I understand.

Ito: **Eˈe, soˈo na n desu. Toˈchi mo semaˈi shi, shiˈgen mo suˈkunaˈi shi soˈre niˈ noˈogyoo-jiˈnkoo mo suˈkunaˈi n desu ne.**

ええ、そうなんです。土地もせまいし、資源も少ないしそれに農業人口も少ないんですね。

Yes, that's right. Our land is small, natural resources are limited and only a small proportion of the population is engaged in agriculture.

Smith: **Koˈogyoˈo-koku da kara, shiˈkata arimaseˈn ne.**

工業国だから、仕方ありませんね。

Japan is an industrialized country, so it can't be helped.

Ito: **Soˈre wa soˈo desu kedo, deˈmo yuˈnyuuhin niˈ taˈyori suˈgite imasu ne.**

それはそうですけど、でも輸入品に頼りすぎていますね。

That's true, but it depends too much on imports.

TEREBI NO RYOORI BANGUMI O MINAGARA
テレビの料理番組を見ながら
Watching a Cooking Program on TV

Kawa: Today, in Lesson 48, Mr. Smith talks about food in Japan. He's been told that a lot of the raw materials for Japanese dishes are imported. Our first key sentence is, "Although it's called Japanese cuisine, I've heard that a lot of the raw materials are imported." "Japanese cuisine," **nihon-ryoori**; "raw materials," **zairyoo**; "imported goods," **yunyuuhin**.

Goto: **Ni⌐hon-ryo⌐ori to itte mo, za⌐iryo⌐o wa yu⌐nyuuhin ga o⌐oi soo desu ne.** 日本料理といっても、材料は輸入品が多いそうですね。

Kawa: **To itte mo** means "although it's called." So, **nihon-ryoori to itte mo** means "although it's called Japanese cuisine." "I've heard that a lot of the raw materials are imported."

Goto: **Za⌐iryo⌐o wa yu⌐nyuuhin ga o⌐oi soo desu ne.** 材料は輸入品が多いそうですね。

Kawa: **Ooi** means "many." **Ooi soo desu** means "I've heard that there are many." Now, the whole sentence again. "Although it's called Japanese cuisine, I've heard that a lot of the raw materials are imported."

Goto: **Ni⌐hon-ryo⌐ori to itte mo, za⌐iryo⌐o wa yu⌐nyuuhin ga o⌐oi soo desu ne.** 日本料理といっても、材料は輸入品が多いそうですね。

Kawa: Now, some substitutions as usual. "Although **sushi** is a Japanese cuisine, I've heard that a lot of the raw materials are imported."

Goto: **Su⌐shi to itte mo, za⌐iryo⌐o wa yu⌐nyuuhin ga o⌐oi soo desu ne.** 寿司といっても、材料は輸入品が多いそうですね。

Kawa: Next, **tenpura**. "Although **tenpura** is a Japanese cuisine, I've heard that a lot of the raw materials are imported."

Goto: **Te⌐npura to itte⌐ mo, za⌐iryo⌐o wa yu⌐nyuuhin ga o⌐oi soo desu ne.** てんぷらといっても、材料は輸入品が多いそうですね。

Kawa: Our second key sentence is, "We shouldn't depend too much on something" or "somebody," featuring **sugiru**, which means "overdo."

Goto: **Ta⌐yorisu⌐gite wa i⌐kenai to omoima⌐su.** 頼りすぎてはいけないと思います。

Kawa: **Tayorisugite wa**, meaning "being too dependent," is a combination of **tayoru**, "depend on," and **sugiru**, "overdo." Let's just remember the expression as it is, **tayorisugite wa**, "being too dependent."

Goto: **Ta⌐yorisu⌐gite wa.** 頼りすぎては

Kawa: "I don't think it is too good...."

Goto: **I⌐kenai to omoima⌐su.** いけないと思います。

Kawa: This literally reads, "I think it's no good...." And the whole sentence: "We shouldn't be too dependent."

Goto: **Ta⌐yorisu⌐gite wa i⌐kenai to omoima⌐su.**
頼りすぎてはいけないと思います。

Kawa: Next, a few substitutions. "We shouldn't eat too much." **Taberu,** "eat," and **sugiru,** "overdo," put together is changed into **tabesugite wa.**

Goto: **Ta⌐besu⌐gite wa i⌐kenai to omoima⌐su.**
食べすぎてはいけないと思います。

Kawa: How about "drinking too much?" "We shouldn't drink too much." **Nomu,** "drink," and **sugiru,** "overdo," into: **nomisugite wa....**

Goto: **No⌐misu⌐gite wa i⌐kenai to omoima⌐su.**
飲みすぎてはいけないと思います。

♪ **Station Break** ⅲⅲⅲ

Kawa: Now, in the second half of this session, we'll discuss each dialogue. Listen to their conversation first.

◆ **Today's Conversation**

S: **Ni⌐hon-ryo⌐ori to itte mo, za⌐iryo⌐o wa yu⌐nyuuhin ga o⌐oi soo desu ne.** 日本料理といっても、材料は輸入品が多いそうですね。

I: **E⌐e, so⌐o na n desu. To⌐chi mo sema⌐i shi, shi⌐gen mo su⌐kuna⌐i shi so⌐re ni⌐ no⌐ogyoo-ji⌐nkoo mo su⌐kuna⌐i n desu ne.**
ええ、そうなんです。土地もせまいし、資源も少ないしそれに農業人口も少ないんですね。

S: **Ko⌐ogyo⌐o-koku da kara, shi⌐kata arimase⌐n ne.**
工業国だから、仕方ありませんね。

I: **So⌐re wa so⌐o desu kedo, de⌐mo yu⌐nyuuhin ni⌐ ta⌐yorisu⌐gite imasu ne.** それはそうですけど、でも輸入品に頼りすぎていますね。

Kawa: Next, you'll listen to its English version.

◆ **Same Conversation in English**

S: Although it's called Japanese cuisine, most of the raw materials are imported, I understand.

I: Yes, that's right. Our land is small, natural resources are limited and only a small proportion of the population is engaged in agriculture.

S: Japan is an industrialized country, so it can't be helped.

I: That's true, but it depends too much on imports.

Kawa: Now each dialogue. We start with "Although it's called Japanese cuisine, I've heard that a lot of the raw materials are imported." This is today's first key sentence.

Goto: **Ni⌈hon-ryo⌉ori to itte mo, za⌈iryo⌉o wa yu⌈nyuuhin ga o⌉oi soo desu ne.** 日本料理といっても、材料は輸入品が多いそうですね。

Kawa: Mrs. Ito admits the fact. "Yes, that's right. Our land is small, natural resources are limited and only a small proportion of the population is engaged in agriculture."

Goto: **E⌉e, so⌉o na n desu. To⌈chi mo sema⌉i shi, shi⌉gen mo su⌈kuna⌉i shi so⌈re ni⌉ no⌈ogyoo-ji⌉nkoo mo su⌈kuna⌉i n desu ne.** ええ、そうなんです。土地もせまいし、資源も少ないしそれに農業人口も少ないんですね。

Kawa: We break it into a few sections. "Yes, that's right."

Goto: **E⌉e, so⌉o na n desu.** ええ、そうなんです。

Kawa: **Ee** is an informal way of saying "yes." She tells him the reason why the Japanese have to import raw materials. "Our land is small." "Land," **tochi.**

Goto: **To⌈chi mo sema⌉i shi.** 土地もせまいし

Kawa: **Semai** means "narrow," which in Japanese goes properly with land, a place, a house and so on, meaning "small." **Shi** at the end practically means "and." Next, "Natural resources are limited." "Natural resources," **shigen**; "is limited," liberally translated as **sukunai.**

Goto: **Shi⌉gen mo su⌈kuna⌉i shi.** 資源も少ないし

Kawa: "…and the farming population is small as well." "Farming population," **noogyo-jinkoo.**

Goto: **So⌈re ni⌉ no⌈ogyoo-ji⌉nkoo mo su⌈kuna⌉i n desu ne.** それに農業人口も少ないんですね。

Kawa: **Sore ni** at the beginning means "and besides." **N desu ne** in **sukunai n desu ne** denotes her emotional emphasis—"is small indeed." Mr. Smith comments on this. "Well, it can't be helped because Japan is an industrialized country." "Industrialized country" is **koogyoo-koku**; "It can't be helped," **shikata arimasen.**

Goto: **Ko⌈ogyo⌉o-koku da kara, shi⌈kata arimase⌉n ne.** 工業国だから、仕方ありませんね。

Kawa: **Koogyoo-koku da kara** means "because Japan is an industrialized country." "Japan" is missing in the sentence as it is obvious. **Shikata arimasen,** "It can't be helped," is an idiomatic expression. Just remember it as it is.

Goto: **Ko⌐ogyo⌐o-koku da kara, shi⌐kata arimase⌐n ne.**
工業国だから、仕方ありませんね。

Kawa: Mrs. Ito agrees to that with some reluctance. "That's true, but it depends too much on imports."

Goto: **So⌐re wa so⌐o desu kedo, de⌐mo yu⌐nyuuhin ni⌐ ta⌐yorisu⌐gite imasu ne.** それはそうですけど、でも輸入品に頼りすぎていますね。

Kawa: **Sore wa soo desu kedo** literally reads "although it may be so." In other words, "That's true, but...."

Goto: **So⌐re wa so⌐o desu kedo.** それはそうですけど、

Kawa: And the next sentence to follow: "But it depends too much on imports." It contains part of our second key sentence, doesn't it?

Goto: **De⌐mo yu⌐nyuuhin ni⌐ ta⌐yorisu⌐gite imasu ne.**
でも輸入品に頼りすぎていますね。

Kawa: **Yunyuuhin ni tayorisugite,** "depending too much on imports." Let's now listen to the whole conversation again.

◆ **Today's Conversation**

S: **Ni⌐hon-ryo⌐ori to itte mo, za⌐iryo⌐o wa yu⌐nyuuhin ga o⌐oi soo desu ne.** 日本料理といっても、材料は輸入品が多いそうですね。

I: **E⌐e, so⌐o na n desu. To⌐chi mo sema⌐i shi, shi⌐gen mo su⌐kuna⌐i shi so⌐re ni⌐ no⌐ogyoo-ji⌐nkoo mo su⌐kuna⌐i n desu ne.**
ええ、そうなんです。土地もせまいし、資源も少ないしそれに農業
人口も少ないんですね。

S: **Ko⌐ogyo⌐o-koku da kara, shi⌐kata arimase⌐n ne.**
工業国だから、仕方ありませんね。

I: **So⌐re wa so⌐o desu kedo, de⌐mo yu⌐nyuuhin ni⌐ ta⌐yorisu⌐gite imasu ne.** それはそうですけど、でも輸入品に頼りすぎていますね。

Kawa: Next, as usual, you'll practice today's vocabulary. Please repeat aloud after Goto-san, who will say each word or phrase twice. First, "raw materials for food."

Goto: **Za⌐iryo⌐o.** 材料

Kawa: "Imported product(s)."

Goto: **Yu⌐nyuuhin.** 輸入品

Kawa: "Farming population."

Goto: **No⌐ogyoo-ji⌐nkoo.** 農業人口

Kawa: "Depend on."

Goto: **Ta⌐yo⌐ru.** 頼る。

Kawa: Now the key sentences again. This time, just listen to Goto-san. The first key sentence: "Although it's called Japanese cuisine, I've heard that a lot of the raw materials are imported."

Goto: **Ni⌈hon-ryo⌉ori to itte mo, za⌈iryo⌉o wa yu⌈nyuuhin ga o⌉oi soo desu ne.** 日本料理といっても、材料は輸入品が多いそうですね。

Kawa: Next, the second key sentence: "We shouldn't be too dependent."

Goto: **Ta⌈yorisu⌉gite wa i⌈kenai to omoima⌉su.**
頼りすぎてはいけないと思います。

Kawa: Now, before we wind up, you'll listen to the whole conversation again.

◆ **Today's Conversation**

S: **Ni⌈hon-ryo⌉ori to itte mo, za⌈iryo⌉o wa yu⌈nyuuhin ga o⌉oi soo desu ne.** 日本料理といっても、材料は輸入品が多いそうですね。

I: **E⌉e, so⌉o na n desu. To⌈chi mo sema⌉i shi, shi⌈gen mo su⌈kuna⌉i shi so⌈re ni⌉ no⌈ogyoo-ji⌉nkoo mo su⌈kuna⌉i n desu ne.**
ええ、そうなんです。土地もせまいし、資源も少ないしそれに農業人口も少ないんですね。

S: **Ko⌈ogyo⌉o-koku da kara, shi⌈kata arimase⌉n ne.**
工業国だから、仕方ありませんね。

I: **So⌈re wa so⌉o desu kedo, de⌉mo yu⌈nyuuhin ni⌉ ta⌈yori⌉sugite imasu ne.** それはそうですけど、でも輸入品に頼りすぎていますね。

Notes

1. X to itte mo ("Although I say X,…")

X **to itte mo** acknowledges X as being a fact but also signals that a corrective statement follows.

> **Yu⌈ube⌉ wa ⌈ha⌉yaku ne⌈ta⌉ to itte mo, ju⌈unijiha⌉n deshita.** ("Last night I went to bed early. I said 'early,' but it was 12:30.")
> **Yo⌉shino-san wa byo⌉oki de⌉su. Byo⌉oki to itte⌉ mo ka⌈isha e⌉ wa i⌈kima⌉shita.** ("Mr. Yoshino is ill. I said 'he is ill,' but he did go to work.")

2. Shi⌈kata (ga) arimasen. ("It can't be helped. There is nothing you can do about it.")

Sometimes this expression is used to defend someone, as in: **Wa⌈ka⌉i n desu kara, shi⌈kata arimase⌉n yo.** ("He is young, so you can't blame him.")

3. ta⌈yorisugi⌉ru ("depends too much")

-su⌈gi⌉ru ("to exceed") is added to the **-ma⌉su** form verb stem or the stem of an adjective (here, you remove the final **-i** to get the stem). With **-na** type nouns, add **-su⌈gi⌉ru** directly to the noun.

Examples: ta⌈bema⌉su   ta⌈besugi⌉ru   ("to eat too much)
             ka⌈ima⌉su   ka⌈isugi⌉ru   ("to buy too much")
             o⌈oki⌉i   o⌈okisugi⌉ru   ("too large")
             wa⌈ka⌉i   wa⌈kasugi⌉ru   ("too young")
             fu⌉ben na   fuben sugi⌉ru   ("too inconvenient")
             ge⌉nki na   ge⌈nki sugi⌉ru   ("too peppy")

Additional Vocabulary

no⌈ogyo⌉o-koku   （農業国）   agricultural country
no⌈oson ji⌉nkoo   （農村人口）   rural population
to⌈shi ji⌉nkoo   （都市人口）   urban population, city population
no⌈oyaku   （農薬）   agricultural chemicals
ga⌈ichuu   （害虫）   harmful insects
ge⌉nryo⌉o   （原料）   raw materials

Exercises

1. Substitute the cue for the underlined word in the model sentence.

   Model Sentence: <u>Ni⌈hon-ryo⌉ori</u> to itte mo, za⌈iryo⌉o wa yu⌈nyuuhin ga o⌉oi soo desu ne.

   1. su⌉shi
   2. te⌈npura
   3. so⌉ba
   4. sho⌈ogatsu no ryo⌉ori
   5. wa⌈shoku

2. Substitute the cue for the underlined word in the model sentence.

   Model Sentence: <u>Ta⌈ka⌉i</u> to itte mo ⌈ta⌉ishita koto wa a⌈rimase⌉n.

   1. mu⌈zukashi⌉i
   2. to⌈oi
   3. ki⌈bishi⌉i
   4. hi⌈ro⌉i
   5. fu⌈ru⌉i

3. Practice dialogue, substituting the cue words for the underlined words in the model.

   Model: ryo⌉ori; ta⌈ka⌉i; ta⌉bete

   A: So⌈no <u>ryo⌉ori</u>, <u>ta⌈ka⌉i</u> n deshoo?
   B: <u>Ta⌈ka⌉i</u> to itte mo ⌈ta⌉ishita koto wa a⌈rimase⌉n.
   A: S⌉oo desu ka. Ja, <u>ta⌉bete</u> mimashoo ka.

1. ho⌐n; mu⌐zukashi⌐i; yo⌐nde
2. mi⌐se⌐; to⌐oi; i⌐tte
3. re⌐nshuu; ki⌐bishi⌐i; ya⌐tte
4. bi⌐yo⌐oin; ta⌐ka⌐i; i⌐tte
5. o⌐sakei tsu⌐yo⌐i; no⌐nde
6. ho⌐teru; ta⌐ka⌐i; to⌐matte
7. ryo⌐ori; mu⌐zukashi⌐i; tsu⌐ku⌐tte

4. Change each sentence so that it ends with -su⌐gita to omoimasu.

Example: Ta⌐yo⌐ru.→Ta⌐yorisu⌐gita to omoimasu.

1. O⌐ishii mono⌐ o ta⌐be⌐ru.
2. Yu⌐ube tomodachi to no⌐mu.
3. No⌐oyaku o tsukau.
4. O⌐yo⌐gu.
5. Te⌐nisu o suru.

In the following sentences, use cho⌐tto [   ]-su⌐gi⌐ru to omoimasu.

Example: Ta⌐ka⌐i.→Cho⌐tto ta⌐kasugi⌐ru to omoimasu.

6. Ko⌐no heya⌐ wa se⌐ma⌐i desu.
7. Ji⌐nkoo ga o⌐oi desu.
8. Shi⌐gen ga su⌐kuna⌐i desu.
9. Ko⌐no kaban wa ooki⌐i desu.
10. A⌐no kissa⌐ten wa ku⌐ra⌐i desu.

5. Making appropriate changes, substitute the cues for the underlined portions of the following dialogue.

A: <u>Yu⌐nyuuhin ni tayo⌐ru</u> no wa shi⌐kata arimase⌐n ne.

B: So⌐re wa so⌐o desu keredo, <u>yu⌐nyuuhin ni tayorisugi⌐ru</u> no wa a⌐mari yo⌐ku ⌐na⌐i to omoimasu ne.

1. a⌐mai mono⌐ o ta⌐be⌐ru
2. sa⌐ke o no⌐mu
3. no⌐oyaku o tsukau
4. no⌐ogyoo ji⌐nkoo ga su⌐kuna⌐i
5. to⌐chi ga taka⌐i

6. Put each of the following clauses at the beginning of the dialogues constructed in Exercise 5.

Example: shi⌐gen ga su⌐kuna⌐i kara

A: <u>Shi⌐gen ga su⌐kuna⌐i kara</u>, yu⌐nyuuhin ni tayo⌐ru no wa shi⌐kata arimase⌐n ne.

B: So⌐re wa so⌐o desu keredo, yu⌐nyuuhin ni tayorisugi⌐ru no wa a⌐mari yo⌐ku ⌐na⌐i to omoimasu ne.

1. pa⌐atii da kara
2. pa⌐atii da kara
3. ga⌐ichuu ga o⌐oi kara
4. ko⌐ogyo⌐o-koku da kara
5. ni⌐ppo⌐n wa se⌐ma⌐i kara

7. Complete each sentence using the most appropriate phrase from the list given below.

1. Ni⌐ppo⌐n wa ko⌐ogyo⌐o-koku da kara,
2. Ni⌐ppo⌐n wa ⌐shi⌐gen ga su⌐kuna⌐i no de,
3. Ko⌐ogyo⌐o-koku to itte mo,
4. Ko⌐no koojo⌐o wa ge⌐nryo⌐o o yu⌐nyuu shite⌐ se⌐ehin o tsuku⌐tte ga⌐ikoku e,
5. Ni⌐hon-ryo⌐ori to itte mo
6. Ni⌐ppo⌐n de wa no⌐oson yo⌐ri ⌐to⌐shi no hoo ga

(a) yu⌐shutsu shite ima⌐su.
(b) za⌐iryo⌐o wa ni⌐hon no ba⌐kari ja a⌐rimase⌐n.
(c) no⌐ogyoo-ji⌐nkoo ga su⌐kuna⌐i desu.
(d) no⌐ogyoo o ya⌐tte iru hito⌐ mo imasu.
(e) ge⌐nryo⌐o o yu⌐nyuu shina⌐kereba na⌐rimase⌐n.
(f) no⌐oyaku o tsukaima⌐su.
(g) ji⌐nkoo ga o⌐oi desu.
(h) no⌐ogyoo-ji⌐nkoo ga ⌐o⌐oi desu.

Answers

1. 1. Su⌐shi to itte mo, zairyo⌐o wa yu⌐nyuuhin ga o⌐oi soo desu ne.
   2. Te⌐npura to itte⌐ mo, zairyo⌐o wa yu⌐nyuuhin ga o⌐oi soo desu ne.
   3. So⌐ba to itte mo, zairyo⌐o wa yu⌐nyuuhin ga o⌐oi soo desu ne.
   4. Sho⌐ogatsu no ryo⌐ori to itte mo, zairyo⌐o wa yu⌐nyuuhin ga o⌐oi soo desu ne.
   5. Wa⌐shoku to itte⌐ mo, zairyo⌐o wa yu⌐nyuuhin ga o⌐oi soo desu ne.

2. 1. Mu⌐zukashi⌐i to itte mo, ta⌐ishita koto wa a⌐rimase⌐n.
   2. To⌐oi⌐ to itte mo, ta⌐ishita koto wa a⌐rimase⌐n.
   3. Ki⌐bishi⌐i to itte mo, ta⌐ishita koto wa a⌐rimase⌐n.
   4. Hi⌐ro⌐i to itte mo, ta⌐ishita koto wa a⌐rimase⌐n.
   5. Fu⌐ru⌐i to itte mo, ta⌐ishita koto wa a⌐rimase⌐n.

3. 1. A: So⌐no ho⌐n, mu⌐zukashi⌐i n deshoo?
      B: Mu⌐zukashi⌐i to itte mo, ta⌐ishita koto wa a⌐rimase⌐n.
      A: So⌐o desu ka. Ja, yo⌐nde mimashoo ka.
      B: E⌐e, ze⌐hi ⌐yo⌐nde mite kudasai.

   2. A: So⌐no mise⌐, to⌐oi⌐ n deshoo?
      B: To⌐oi⌐ to itte mo, ta⌐ishita koto wa a⌐rimase⌐n.
      A: So⌐o desu ka. Ja, i⌐tte mimasho⌐o ka.
      B: E⌐e, ze⌐hi i⌐tte mi⌐te kudasai.

3. A: So⌐no renshuu⌐, ki⌐bishi⌐i n deshoo?
   B: Ki⌐bishi⌐i to itte mo, ta⌐ishita koto wa a⌐rimase⌐n.
   A: So⌐o desu ka. Ja, ya⌐tte mimasho⌐o ka.
   B: E⌐e, ze⌐hi ya⌐tte mi⌐te kudasai.

4. A: So⌐no biyo⌐oin, ta⌐ka⌐i n deshoo?
   B: Ta⌐ka⌐i to itte mo, ta⌐ishita koto wa a⌐rimase⌐n.
   A: So⌐o desu ka. Ja, i⌐tte mimasho⌐o ka.
   B: E⌐e, ze⌐hi i⌐tte mi⌐te kudasai.

5. A: So⌐no osake⌐, tsu⌐yo⌐i n deshoo?
   B: Tsu⌐yo⌐i to itte mo, ta⌐ishita koto wa a⌐rimase⌐n.
   A: So⌐o desu ka. Ja, no⌐nde mimashoo ka.
   B: E⌐e, ze⌐hi no⌐nde mite kudasai.

6. A: So⌐no ho⌐teru ta⌐ka⌐i n deshoo?
   B: Ta⌐ka⌐i to itte mo, ta⌐ishita koto wa a⌐rimase⌐n.
   A: So⌐o desu ka. Ja, to⌐matte mimasho⌐o ka.
   B: E⌐e, ze⌐hi to⌐matte mi⌐te kudasai.

7. A: So⌐no ryo⌐ori, mu⌐zukashi⌐i n deshoo?
   B: Mu⌐zukashi⌐i to itte mo, ta⌐ishita koto wa a⌐rimase⌐n.
   A: So⌐o desu ka. Ja, tsu⌐ku⌐tte mimashoo ka.
   B: E⌐e, ze⌐hi tsu⌐ku⌐tte mite kudasai.

4. 1. O⌐ishii mono⌐ o ta⌐besu⌐gita to omoimasu.
   2. Yu⌐ube tomodachi to⌐ no⌐misu⌐gita to omoimasu.
   3. No⌐oyaku o tsukaisu⌐gita to omoimasu.
   4. O⌐yogisu⌐gita to omoimasu.
   5. Te⌐nisu o shisu⌐gita to omoimasu.
   6. Ko⌐no heya⌐ wa ⌐cho⌐tto se⌐masugi⌐ru to omoimasu.
   7. Ji⌐nkoo ga cho⌐tto o⌐osugi⌐ru to omoimasu.
   8. Shi⌐gen ga ⌐cho⌐tto su⌐kunasugi⌐ru to omoimasu.
   9. Ko⌐no kaban wa cho⌐tto o⌐okisugi⌐ru to omoimasu.
   10. A⌐no kissa⌐ten wa ⌐cho⌐tto ku⌐rasugi⌐ru to omoimasu.

5. 1. A: A⌐mai mono⌐ o ta⌐be⌐ru no wa shi⌐kata arimase⌐n ne.
      B: So⌐re wa so⌐o desu keredo, a⌐mai mono⌐ o ta⌐besugi⌐ru no wa, a⌐mari yo⌐ku ⌐na⌐i to omoimasu.

   2. A: Sa⌐ke o no⌐mu no wa shi⌐kata arimase⌐n ne.
      B: So⌐re wa so⌐o desu keredo, sa⌐ke o nomisugi⌐ru no wa, a⌐mari yo⌐ku ⌐na⌐i to omoimasu.

   3. A: No⌐oyaku o tsukau⌐ no wa shi⌐kata arimase⌐n ne.
      B: So⌐re wa so⌐o desu keredo, no⌐oyaku o tsukaisugi⌐ru no wa, a⌐mari yo⌐ku ⌐na⌐i to omoimasu.

   4. A: No⌐ogyoo ji⌐nkoo ga su⌐kuna⌐i no wa shi⌐kata arimase⌐n ne.
      B: So⌐re wa so⌐o desu keredo, no⌐ogyoo ji⌐nkoo ga su⌐kunasugi⌐ru no wa, a⌐mari yo⌐ku ⌐na⌐i to omoimasu.

   5. A: To⌐chi ga taka⌐i no wa shi⌐kata arimase⌐n ne.
      B: So⌐re wa so⌐o desu keredo, to⌐chi ga takasugi⌐ru no wa, a⌐mari yo⌐ku ⌐na⌐i to omoimasu.

7. 1. (c)   4. (a)
   2. (e)   5. (b)
   3. (d)   6. (g)

AˈKIHAˈBARA DE DEˈNKI SEˈEHIN O KAU

秋葉原で電気製品を買う

Buying Electric Appliances in Akihabara

Today's Conversation

Smith: **Teˈrebi mo ˈraˈjio mo paˈsokon moˈ, waˈriai yasuˈi desu ne.**
テレビもラジオもパソコンも、わりあい安いですね。
Television sets, radios, personal computers—they are all relatively cheap.

Ito: **Eˈe, deˈpaˈato yori heˈekinˈ saˈn-wari guˈrai yaˈsuˈi desu yo.**
ええ、デパートより平均3割ぐらい安いですよ。
Yes, everything is about 30 percent cheaper than at a department store.

Smith: **Naˈni o kaˈttaˈra ˈiˈi ka, maˈyoimaˈsu ne.**
何を買ったらいいか、まよいますね。
It's difficult to know what to buy.

Ito: **Oˈtoko no oko-san niˈ wa, koˈnna chiisaˈi ˈraˈjio wa ˈdoˈo desu ka.**
男のお子さんには、こんな小さいラジオはどうですか。
How about a small radio like this for your son?

Smith: **Iˈi desu ne. Oˈnnaˈ no ko ni wa, koˈnoˈ kaˈwaiˈi toˈkee ni shimashoˈo. Teˈrebi mo kaˈitaˈi keredo, oˈokisugi-maˈsu ne.**
いいですね。女の子には、このかわいい時計にしましょう。テレビも買いたいけれど、大きすぎますね。

Fine. And I will buy this cute watch for my daughter. I would like to buy a TV set, too, but they are too big.

Ito: **Ko⌐gata no⌐ mo a⌐rima⌐su yo. Ta⌐kasa ju⌐ugosenchi gu⌐rai no. Mo⌐o suko⌐shi sa⌐gashimasho⌐o.**

小型のもありますよ。高さ１５センチぐらいの。もう少しさがしましょう。

You can find a small one, too—about 15 centimeters high. Let's look some more.

Smith: **Do⌐ko no mi⌐se⌐ de mo, sho⌐ohin o ⌐ki⌐ree ni na⌐rabe-ta⌐ri, o⌐oki na ⌐ko⌐e de o⌐kyaku o yonda⌐ri, se⌐nden ga⌐ ta⌐ihen de⌐su ne.**

どこの店でも、商品をきれいに並べたり、大きな声でお客を呼んだり、宣伝がたいへんですね。

They work hard at promotion at every store, arranging their merchandise in an attractive way, calling out to customers loudly.

Ito: **Mi⌐se⌐ ga ⌐o⌐oi kara kyo⌐osoo ga⌐ ki⌐bishi⌐i n deshoo ne. De⌐mo ne⌐dan wa⌐ a⌐mari kawaranai yo⌐o desu yo.**

店が多いから競争がきびしいんでしょうね。でも値段はあまり変わらないようですよ。

There are so many shops that the competition is severe. But they seem to sell things at about the same prices.

Smith: **To⌐ori no muko⌐o ni mo de⌐pa⌐ato no yoo ni ⌐o⌐oki na mi⌐se⌐ ga a⌐rima⌐su ne. I⌐tte mimasho⌐o ka.**

通りの向こうにもデパートのように大きな店がありますね。行ってみましょうか。

There's a store as large as a department store across the street. Shall we go and look there?

AKIHABARA DE DENKI SEEHIN O KAU
秋葉原で電気製品を買う
Buying Electric Appliances in Akihabara

Kawa: Today, in Lesson 49, you'll find no new sentence patterns, so we won't explain much of the details. Now, Mr. Smith goes to Akihabara with Mr. Ito to buy electric appliances. He finds a lot of attractive shops there selling electric appliances of all sorts. Our first key sentence is, "I would like to buy a TV set, too, but they're too big, aren't they?"

Goto: **Te⌐rebi mo ka⌐ita⌐i keredo, o⌐okisugima⌐su ne.**
テレビも買いたいけれど、大きすぎますね。

Kawa: "I would like to buy a TV set, too, but…."

Goto: **Te⌐rebi mo ka⌐ita⌐i keredo,** テレビも買いたいけれど、

Kawa: "They're too big, aren't they?"

Goto: **O⌐okisugima⌐su ne.** 大きすぎますね。

Kawa: Let's replace the TV set with "personal computer," or **pasokon** in spoken Japanese. "I would like to buy a personal computer, too, but they're too expensive, aren't they? "Expensive," **takai**.

Goto: **Pa⌐sokon mo kaita⌐i keredo, ta⌐kasugima⌐su ne.**
パソコンも買いたいけれど、高すぎますね。

Kawa: Next, the second key sentence, "There are small ones, too."

Goto: **Ko⌐gata no⌐ mo a⌐rima⌐su yo.** 小型のもありますよ。

Kawa: **Kogata** means "small." **Kogata no** means "small ones." Let's replace the small ones with "cheap ones," which is **yasui no**.

Goto: **Ya⌐su⌐i no mo a⌐rima⌐su yo.** 安いのもありますよ。

Kawa: **Yasui no mo**, "a cheap one, too." Our third key sentence is, "There's a big store like a department store." "A big store," **ooki na mise**.

Goto: **De⌐pa⌐ato no yoo ni ⌐o⌐oki na mi⌐se⌐ ga a⌐rima⌐su ne.**
デパートのように大きな店がありますね。

Kawa: Let's replace "the department store" with "a supermarket," which we simply call **suupaa** in spoken Japanese.

Goto: **Su⌐upaa no yoo ni ⌐o⌐oki na mi⌐se⌐ ga a⌐rima⌐su ne.**
スーパーのように大きな店がありますね。

♪ **Station Break** 〰〰〰〰〰〰〰〰〰〰〰〰〰〰〰〰〰〰〰〰〰〰〰〰〰〰〰

Kawa: In the second half of this program, we'll discuss each dialogue as usual. Listen to the whole conversation first.

◆ **Today's Conversation**

S: **Te⌐rebi mo ⌐ra⌐jio mo pa⌐sokon mo⌐, wa⌐riai yasu⌐i desu ne.**
テレビもラジオもパソコンも、わりあい安いですね。

I: **E⌐e, de⌐pa⌐ato yori he⌐ekin⌐ sa⌐n-wari gu⌐rai ya⌐su⌐i desu yo.**
ええ、デパートより平均3割ぐらい安いですよ。

S: **Na⌐ni o ka⌐tta⌐ra ⌐i⌐i ka, ma⌐yoima⌐su ne.**
何を買ったらいいか、まよいますね。

I: **O⌐toko no oko-san ni⌐ wa, ko⌐nna chiisa⌐i ⌐ra⌐jio wa ⌐do⌐o desu ka.**
男のお子さんには、こんな小さいラジオはどうですか。

S: Iˈi desu ne. Oˈnnaˈ no ko ni wa, koˈnoˈ kaˈwaiˈi toˈkee ni shimashoˈo. Teˈrebi mo kaˈitaˈi keredo, oˈokisugimaˈsu ne.
いいですね。女の子には、このかわいい時計にしましょう。テレビも買いたいけれど、大きすぎますね。

I: Koˈgata noˈ mo aˈrimaˈsu yo. Taˈkasa juˈugosenchi guˈrai no. Moˈo sukoˈshi saˈgashimashoˈo.
小型のもありますよ。高さ15センチぐらいの。もう少しさがしましょう。

S: Doˈko no miˈseˈ de mo, shoˈohin o ˈkiˈree ni naˈrabetaˈri, oˈoki na ˈkoˈe de oˈkyaku o yondaˈri, seˈnden gaˈ taˈihen deˈsu ne.
どこの店でも、商品をきれいに並べたり、大きな声でお客を呼んだり、宣伝がたいへんですね。

I: Miˈseˈ ga ˈoˈoi kara kyoˈosoo gaˈ kiˈbishiˈi n deshoo ne. Deˈmo neˈdan waˈ aˈmari kawaranai yoˈo desu yo.
店が多いから競争がきびしいんでしょうね。でも値段はあまり変わらないようですよ。

S: Toˈori no mukoˈo ni mo deˈpaˈato no yoo ni ˈoˈoki na miˈseˈ ga aˈrimaˈsu ne. Iˈtte mimashoˈo ka.
通りの向こうにもデパートのように大きな店がありますね。行ってみましょうか。

Kawa: Next, you'll listen to its English version.

◆ Same Conversation in English

S: Television sets, radios, personal computers—they are all relatively cheap.

I: Yes, everything is about 30 percent cheaper than at a department store.

S: It's difficult to know what to buy.

I: How about a small radio like this for your son?

S: Fine. And I will buy this cute watch for my daughter. I would like to buy a TV set, too, but they are too big.

I: You can find a small one, too—about 15 centimeters high. Let's look some more.

S: They work hard at promotion at every store, arranging their merchandise in an attractive way, calling out to customers loudly.

I: There are so many shops that the competition is severe. But they seem to sell things at about the same prices.

S: There's a store as large as a department store across the street. Shall we go and look there?

Kawa: Now we study each dialogue. Mr. Smith is happy to find everything at the shops rather cheap. "Television sets, radios and personal computers—they are all relatively cheap."

Goto: **Te⌐rebi mo ⌐ra⌐jio mo pa⌐sokon mo⌐, wa⌐riai yasu⌐i desu ne.**
テレビもラジオもパソコンも、わりあい安いですね。

Kawa: **Wariai** means "relatively;" **yasui,** "cheap." Mr. Ito agrees. "Yes, everything is about 30 percent cheaper than at a department store."

Goto: **E⌐e, de⌐pa⌐ato yori he⌐ekin⌐ sa⌐n-wari gu⌐rai ya⌐su⌐i desu yo.**
ええ、デパートより平均３割ぐらい安いですよ。

Kawa: **Heekin** means "average" but here, "on the average." Mr. Smith wonders what to buy. He says, "It's hard to decide what to buy, isn't it?"

Goto: **Na⌐ni o ka⌐tta⌐ra ⌐i⌐i ka, ma⌐yoima⌐su ne.**
何を買ったらいいか、まよいますね。

Kawa: **Mayoimasu** means "hesitate." Mr. Ito makes a suggestion. "How about a small radio like this for your son?"

Goto: **O⌐toko no oko-san ni⌐ wa, ko⌐nna chiisa⌐i ⌐ra⌐jio wa ⌐do⌐o desu ka.**
男のお子さんには、こんな小さいラジオはどうですか。

Kawa: **Otoko no oko-san ni wa** is a polite "for your son." "That's good," agrees Mr. Smith, "and I'll buy this cute watch for my daughter."

Goto: **I⌐i desu ne. O⌐nna⌐ no ko ni wa, ko⌐no⌐ ka⌐wai⌐i to⌐kee ni shimasho⌐o.**
いいですね。女の子には、このかわいい時計にしましょう。

Kawa: He's also interested in a TV set and says, "I would like to buy a TV set, too, but they are too big."

Goto: **Te⌐rebi mo ka⌐ita⌐i keredo, o⌐okisugima⌐su ne.**
テレビも買いたいけれど、大きすぎますね。

Kawa: This is our first key sentence. Mr. Ito makes a suggestion, which is our second key sentence. "There're small ones, too." "Small ones," **kogata no.**

Goto: **Ko⌐gata no⌐ mo a⌐rima⌐su yo.** 小型のもありますよ。

Kawa: **Mo** in **no mo** means "also" or "too." "Ones about 15 centimeters high."

Goto: **Ta⌐kasa ju⌐ugosenchi gu⌐rai no.** 高さ１５センチぐらいの。

Kawa: "Let's look around a little more," says Mr. Ito.

Goto: **Mo⌐o suko⌐shi sa⌐gashimasho⌐o.** もう少しさがしましょう。

Kawa: Mr. Smith marvels at what he sees there. "They work hard at promotion at every store, arranging their merchandise in an attractive way, calling out loudly to customers." A bit long. Let's break it into sections. "They work hard at promotion."

Goto: **Se⌐nden ga┘ ta⌐ihen de┘su ne.** 宣伝がたいへんですね。

Kawa: **Senden,** "advertisement;" **taihen desu,** "it's hard" or "it's tough." The next phrase to follow: "at every shop."

Goto: **Do┘ko no mi⌐se┘ de mo.** どこの店でも、

Kawa: "Arranging their merchandise in an attractive way." "Arrange," **naraberu;** "merchandise," **shoohin;** "in an attractive way," **kiree ni.**

Goto: **Sho┘ohin o⌐ki┘ree ni na⌐rabeta┘ri.** 商品をきれいに並べたり、

Kawa: "Calling out loudly to customers."

Goto: **O┘oki na ⌐ko┘e de o⌐kyaku o yonda┘ri.** 大きな声でお客を呼んだり、

Kawa: **Ooki na koe de,** "loudly;" **okyaku,** "customers;" **-dari** or **-tari** means practically "and." Mr. Ito comments, "There are so many shops that the competition is severe. But they seem to sell things at about the same prices." "Competition," **kyosoo;** "severe," **kibishii;** "price," **nedan.**

Goto: **Mi⌐se┘ ga ⌐o┘oi kara kyo⌐osoo ga┘ ki⌐bishi┘i n deshoo ne. De┘mo ne⌐dan wa┘ a⌐mari kawaranai yo┘o desu yo.**
店が多いから競争がきびしいんでしょうね。でも値段はあまり変わらないようですよ。

Kawa: Mr. Smith has found another big store and says, "There's a big store like a department store across the street."

Goto: **To⌐ori no muko┘o ni mo de⌐pa┘ato no yoo ni ⌐o┘oki na mi⌐se┘ ga a⌐rima┘su ne.**
通りの向こうにもデパートのように大きな店がありますね。

Kawa: **Toori no mukoo ni mo,** "also across the street." He says, " Shall we go and have a look there?"

Goto: **I⌐tte mimasho┘o ka.** 行ってみましょうか。

Kawa: Now today's vocabulary. Please repeat aloud after Goto-san, who'll say each word or phrase twice. First, "30 percent."

Goto: **Sa┘n-wari.** ３割

Kawa: "Advertisement."

Goto: **Se⌐nden.** 宣伝

Kawa: "Competition."

Goto: **Kyo⌐osoo.** 競争

Kawa: "Customer."

Goto: **O⌐kyaku.** お客

Kawa: Now, you'll review today's key sentences. Just listen to Goto-san. Today's first key sentence: "I would like to buy a TV set, too, but they're too big."

Goto: **Te┘rebi mo ka⌐ita┘i keredo, o⌐okisugima┘su ne.**
テレビも買いたいけれど、大きすぎますね。

Kawa: The second key sentence: "There are small ones, too."

Goto: **Ko⌐gata no⌐ mo a⌐rima⌐su yo.** 小型のもありますよ。

Kawa: Then, the third key sentence: "There's a big store like a department store."

Goto: **De⌐pa⌐ato no yoo ni ⌐o⌐oki na mi⌐se⌐ ga a⌐rima⌐su ne.**
        デパートのように大きな店がありますね。

Kawa: Now, before we wind up, let's listen to the whole dialogue again.

◆ **Today's Conversation**

S: **Te⌐rebi mo ⌐ra⌐jio mo pa⌐sokon mo⌐, wa⌐riai yasu⌐i desu ne.**
     テレビもラジオもパソコンも、わりあい安いですね。

I: **E⌐e, de⌐pa⌐ato yori he⌐ekin⌐ sa⌐n-wari gu⌐rai ya⌐su⌐i desu yo.**
     ええ、デパートより平均３割ぐらい安いですよ。

S: **Na⌐ni o ka⌐tta⌐ra ⌐i⌐i ka, ma⌐yoima⌐su ne.**
     何を買ったらいいか、まよいますね。

I: **O⌐toko no oko-san ni⌐ wa, ko⌐nna chiisa⌐i ⌐ra⌐jio wa ⌐do⌐o desu ka.**
     男のお子さんには、こんな小さいラジオはどうですか。

S: **I⌐i desu ne. O⌐nna⌐ no ko ni wa, ko⌐no⌐ ka⌐wai⌐i to⌐kee ni shimasho⌐o.
     Te⌐rebi mo ka⌐ita⌐i keredo, o⌐okisugima⌐su ne.**
     いいですね。女の子には、このかわいい時計にしましょう。テレビ
     も買いたいけれど、大きすぎますね。

I: **Ko⌐gata no⌐ mo a⌐rima⌐su yo. Ta⌐kasa ju⌐ugosenchi gu⌐rai no. Mo⌐o
     suko⌐shi sa⌐gashimasho⌐o.**
     小型のもありますよ。高さ１５センチぐらいの。もう少しさがしま
     しょう。

S: **Do⌐ko no mi⌐se⌐ de mo, sho⌐ohin o⌐ki⌐ree ni na⌐rabeta⌐ri, o⌐oki na
     ⌐ko⌐e de o⌐kyaku o yonda⌐ri, se⌐nden ga⌐ ta⌐ihen de⌐su ne.**
     どこの店でも、商品をきれいに並べたり、大きな声でお客を呼んだ
     り、宣伝がたいへんですね。

I: **Mi⌐se⌐ ga ⌐o⌐oi kara kyo⌐osoo ga⌐ ki⌐bishi⌐i n deshoo ne. De⌐mo
     ne⌐dan wa⌐ a⌐mari kawaranai yo⌐o desu yo.**
     店が多いから競争がきびしいんでしょうね。でも値段はあまり変わ
     らないようですよ。

S: **To⌐ori no muko⌐o ni mo de⌐pa⌐ato no yoo ni ⌐o⌐oki na mi⌐se⌐ ga
     a⌐rima⌐su ne. I⌐tte mimasho⌐o ka.**
     通りの向こうにもデパートのように大きな店がありますね。行っ
     てみましょうか。

Notes

1. na⌐ni o ka⌐tta⌐ra ⌐i⌐i ka

Na⌐ni o ka⌐tta⌐ra ⌐i⌐i deshoo ka. Literally this sentence means "If I buy what, is it alright, I wonder." So, it means "What should I buy?"

The **-tara** form is made as follows: With verbs and adjectives, add **-ra** to the informal past tense.

Examples:	"go"	i⌐tta⌐ra
	"see"	mi⌐tara
	"drink"	no⌐ndara
	"do"	shi⌐ta⌐ra
	"big"	o⌐okikattara
	"expensive"	ta⌐kakattara
	"interesting"	o⌐moshi⌐rokattara

With noun and **na**-type adjectives, add **-n⌐ara** or **-da⌐ttara**.

Examples:	"rain"	a⌐me nara or a⌐me dattara
	"Japanese"	Ni⌐pponji⌐n nara or Ni⌐pponjin⌐ dattara
	"beautiful"	ki⌐ree nara or ki⌐ree dattara

More examples: **Do⌐ko de ka⌐tta⌐ra ⌐i⌐i deshoo ka.** ("Where should I buy it?")
Da⌐re ni kiitara ⌐i⌐i deshoo ka. ("Whom should I ask?")
I⌐tsu denwa shitara ⌐i⌐i deshoo ka. ("When should I call?")
Do⌐no shinbun o kattara ⌐i⌐i deshoo ka. ("Which newspaper should I buy?")

Answers to these questions might be:

To⌐kee o katta⌐ra ⌐i⌐i deshoo. ("How about buying a watch?")
A⌐kiha⌐bara de ka⌐tta⌐ra ⌐i⌐i deshoo. ("How about buying in Akihabara?")
Ya⌐mamoto-san ni kiita⌐ra ⌐i⌐i deshoo. ("How about asking Mr. Yamamoto?")
Ha⌐chiji go⌐ro de⌐nwa shita⌐ra ⌐i⌐i deshoo. ("How about calling him at about 8 o'clock?")
Ko⌐no shinbun o katta⌐ra ⌐i⌐i deshoo. ("How about buying this newspaper?")

2. <u>De⌐pa⌐ato no yoo ni ⌐o⌐oki na mi⌐se⌐ ga arimasu ne.</u>

X **no yoo ni** is an adverbial phrase that means "like X." Do not confuse this phrase with X **no yoo na**, which is an adjectival phrase, used to modify nouns. <u>Sa⌐kura no yo⌐o na</u> **hana desu.** ("It's a flower like a cherry blossom.") <u>Sa⌐kura no yo⌐o na</u> is an adjectival phrase qualifying **hana**, a noun. <u>Ka⌐wa no yo⌐o ni miemasu.</u> ("It looks like a river.") <u>Ka⌐wa no yo⌐o ni</u> is an adverbial phrase qualifying **mi⌐ema⌐su**, a verb.

Examples: **O⌐nna no yo⌐o ni ⌐ki⌐ree na ka⌐buki ya⌐kusha desu.**
O⌐sumoo-san no yo⌐o ni fu⌐to⌐tta hito desu.
Ya⌐ma no na⌐ka no yoo ni ⌐shi⌐zuka na otaku desu.

Exercises

1. Substituting the cues for the underlined portions (and making necesary changes), practice the following dialogue.

Example: na｜ni o kau; chi⌈isa｜i ⌈ra｜jio

A: <u>Na｜ni o kattara</u> ii ka, ma⌈yo｜tte iru n desu ga.
B: <u>Chi⌈isa｜i ⌈ra｜jio o kattara</u> i⌈ka｜ga desu ka.
A: I⌈i desu ne. <u>Chi⌈isa｜i ⌈ra｜jio</u> ni shimashoo.

1. do｜ko e iku; Ha⌈kone
2. do｜nna omiyage o kau; se⌈nsu
3. i｜tsu hanasu; o⌈hiruyasumi
4. do｜no pasokon o kau; ko⌈no atarashi｜i no
5. na｜ni o miru; To⌈okyoo ta｜waa ya de⌈pa｜ato nado

2. According to "Today's Conversation," answer the following questions in Japanese.

1. Su｜misu-san to I⌈too-san wa do｜ko ni imasu ka.
2. A⌈kiha｜bara no mise to de⌈pa｜ato to, do｜chira no hoo ga ya⌈su｜i desu ka.
3. Do⌈no gurai yasu｜i desu ka.
4. Su｜misu-san wa ⌈na｜ze ma⌈yo｜u no desu ka.
5. I⌈too-san wa na｜ni ga ii to i⌈ima｜shita ika.
6. Su｜misu-san wa ko⌈domo｜tachi ni ⌈na｜ni o kau koto ni shimashita ka.
7. Fu⌈tari｜ wa ⌈do｜nna terebi o sagashimasu ka.
8. Mi⌈se no hito｜tachi wa se⌈nden ni do｜nna koto o shite imasu ka.
9. Na｜ze kyoosoo ga ki⌈bishi｜i n desu ka.
10. Ne⌈dan wa｜ chi⌈gaima｜su ka.
11. Ko⌈re kara futari｜ wa ⌈do｜ko e ikimasu ka.

3. Put into Japanese.

1. The price of this shop is cheaper by about 30 percent than that of a department store.
2. I'd like to buy a small-sized TV set.
3. A: There is a store as large as a department store across the street.
   B: That's right. Shall we go and look there?
4. A: This bag is nice. Both the shape and the color are nice, but it is a bit too large.
   B: How about this small one?
   A: Oh, that's a bit too small. Let's look some more.
5. A: Which personal computer should I buy?
   B: How about this one? I have the same one. It's good and relatively cheap.

6. A: Are you going out tonight?
   B: If it rains, I won't go out.

7. If it is cheap, I will buy it.

8. A: Do you have time today?
   B: Yes, if it's in the afternoon, I have time.

Answers

1. 1. A: Do⌐ko e ittara ii ka, ma⌐yo⌐tte iru n desu ga.
      B: Ha⌐kone e itta⌐ra, i⌐ka⌐ga desu ka.
      A: I⌐i desu ne. Ha⌐kone ni shimasho⌐o.

   2. A: Do⌐nna omiyage o ka⌐tta⌐ra ii ka, ma⌐yo⌐tte iru n desu ga.
      B: Se⌐nsu o katta⌐ra, i⌐ka⌐ga desu ka.
      A: I⌐i desu ne. Se⌐nsu ni shimasho⌐o.

   3. A: I⌐tsu hanashitara ii ka, ma⌐yo⌐tte iru n desu ga.
      B: O⌐hiruya⌐sumi ni hanashitara i⌐ka⌐ga desu ka.
      A: I⌐i desu ne. O⌐hiruya⌐sumi ni shimasho⌐o.

   4. A: Do⌐no pasokon o kattara ii ka, ma⌐yo⌐tte iru n desu ga.
      B: Ko⌐no atarashi⌐i no o kattara i⌐ka⌐ga desu ka.
      A: I⌐i desu ne. Ko⌐no atarashi⌐i no ni shimasho⌐o.

   5. A: Na⌐ni o mitara ii ka, ma⌐yo⌐tte iru n desu ga.
      B: To⌐okyoo ta⌐waa ya de⌐pa⌐too nado o mitara i⌐ka⌐ga desu ka.
      A: I⌐i desu ne. To⌐okyoo ta⌐waa ya de⌐pa⌐too nado ni shimasho⌐o.

2. 1. A⌐kiha⌐bara ni imasu.
   2. A⌐kiha⌐bara (no mise) no hoo ga ya⌐su⌐i desu.
   3. He⌐ekin⌐ sa⌐n-wari gu⌐rai ya⌐su⌐i desu.
   4. I⌐roiro a⌐ru kara ⌐na⌐ni o kattara ii ka ma⌐yo⌐tte shimau n desu.
   5. O⌐toko⌐ no ko ni wa chi⌐isa⌐i ⌐ra⌐jio ga ii daroo to i⌐ima⌐shita.
   6. O⌐toko⌐ no ko ni wa chi⌐isa⌐i ⌐ra⌐jio o, o⌐nn⌐a no ko ni wa (ka⌐wai⌐i) to⌐kee o kau koto⌐ ni shi⌐ma⌐shita.
   7. Ta⌐kasa ju⌐ugosenchi gu⌐rai no ko⌐gata no te⌐rebi desu.
   8. Sho⌐ohin o ⌐ki⌐ree ni na⌐rabeta⌐ri, o⌐oki na ⌐ko⌐e de o⌐kyaku o yonda⌐ri shite imasu.
   9. (O⌐naji yo⌐o na) mi⌐se⌐ ga ⌐o⌐oi kara desu.
   10. I⌐ie, ne⌐dan wa amari kawarimase⌐n.
   11. To⌐ori no mukoo no⌐ de⌐pa⌐ato no yoo ni ⌐o⌐oki na mi⌐se⌐ ni ikimasu.

3. 1. Ko⌐no mise no nedan wa⌐ de⌐pa⌐ato yori sa⌐n-wari gu⌐rai ya⌐su⌐i desu.

   2. Ko⌐gata no te⌐rebi o ka⌐ita⌐i n desu ga.

   3. A: To⌐ori no mukoo ni⌐ de⌐pa⌐ato no yoo ni ⌐o⌐oki na mi⌐se⌐ ga arimasu ne.
      B: E⌐e, a⌐soko e itte mimasho⌐o ka.

   4. A: Ko⌐no kaban, i⌐i desu ne. Ka⌐tachi mo⌐ i⌐ro⌐ mo ⌐i⌐i desu kedo, cho⌐tto o⌐okisugima⌐su ne.
      B: Ko⌐no chiisa⌐i no wa ⌐do⌐o desu ka.
      A: A⌐a, so⌐re wa chiisasugima⌐su. Mo⌐o suko⌐shi mi⌐masho⌐o.

   5. A: Do⌐no pasokon o kattara ⌐i⌐i deshoo ka.
      B: Ko⌐re wa do⌐o desu ka. Wa⌐tashi mo onaji⌐ no ga a⌐rima⌐su ga, ⌐i⌐i desu shi, wa⌐riai yasu⌐i desu yo.

6. A: Koˈnban, deˈkakemaˈsu ka.
   B: Aˈme ga futtara, deˈkakemaseˈn.

7. Yaˈsukattara kaˈimaˈsu.

8. A: Kyoˈo, jiˈkan, arimaˈsu ka.
   B: Eˈe, goˈgo nara (or goˈgo dattara) jiˈkan ga arimaˈsu.

LESSON
50

Iᒋᴛᴏᴏᒋ-KE DE Oᒋᴡᴀᴋᴀʀᴇ NO KAᒋɪ
伊藤家でお別れの会
Farewell Party at the Itos'

Today's Conversation

Ito:	**Suᒋmisu-san, koᒋre, oᒋkusan ni aᒋgete kudasaimaseᒋn ka. Fuᒋroshiki deᒋsu.**
	スミスさん、これ、奥さんにあげて下さいませんか。ふろしきです。
	Would you give this to your wife? It's a furoshiki.
Smith:	**Koᒋre wa naᒋn ni tsuᒋkauᒋ n desu ka.**
	これは何に使うんですか。
	What is this used for?
Ito:	**Hiᒋrogereᒋba moᒋnoᒋ o tsuᒋtsuᒋmu no ni tsuᒋkaeruᒋ shi, kaᒋbe ni kakeᒋreba, kaᒋzari niᒋ mo narimasu.**
	広げればものを包むのに使えるし、壁にかければ、飾りにもなります。
	You can use it to wrap things in when you spread it out, and you can use it as a decoration if you hang it on the wall.
Smith:	**Aᒋa, soᒋo desu ka. Taᒋtameᒋba ᒋchiᒋisaku naru kara ᒋbeᒋnri desu ne.**
	ああ、そうですか。たためば小さくなるから便利ですね。
	Is that right? It is handy because it becomes small if you fold it up.

ITOO-KE DE OWAKARE NO KAI
伊藤家でお別れの会
Farewell Party at the Itos'

Kawa: Today, in Lesson 50, we hear Mr. Smith and Mrs. Ito at her home, where the Itos are holding a farewell party for Mr. Smith. Mrs. Ito has got a present for him. She asks him, "Would you give this to your wife?" Our first key sentence.

Goto: **Ko⌈re, o⌉kusan ni a⌈gete kudaisaimase⌉n ka.**
これ、奥さんにあげて下さいませんか。

Kawa: **-te kudaisaimasen ka** makes it very polite. "Please give this to your wife" in simpler terms would be:

Goto: **Ko⌈re, o⌉kusan ni a⌈gete kudasa⌉i.** 奥さんにあげて下さい。

Kawa: This is reasonably polite, but you can be even more so by adding…

Goto: **-masen ka.** ませんか。

Kawa: …to **agete kudasai.** Listen again.

Goto: **Ko⌈re, o⌉kusan ni a⌈gete kudaisaimase⌉n ka.**
これ、奥さんにあげて下さいませんか。

Kawa: Suppose you've got a present for someone's husband:

Goto: **Ko⌈re, go⌈shu⌉jin ni a⌈gete kudaisaimase⌉n ka.**
これ、ご主人にあげて下さいませんか。

Kawa: **Goshujin** means someone's "husband." "To your husband" is:

Goto: **Go⌈shu⌉jin ni.** ご主人に

Kawa: "Would you please give this to your husband?"

Goto: **Ko⌈re, go⌈shu⌉jin ni a⌈gete kudaisaimase⌉n ka.**
これ、ご主人にあげて下さいませんか。

Kawa: How about asking someone to use something? **Tsukatte kudasai** means "Please use this." You want to make it sound even more polite.

Goto: **Ko⌈re, tsu⌈katte kudaisaimase⌉n ka.** これ、使って下さいませんか。

Kawa: Mrs. Ito's present for Mrs. Smith is **furoshiki,** a useful Japanese wrapping cloth. "We use it to wrap things in," she says, our second key sentence.

Goto: **Mo⌈no⌉ o tsu⌈tsu⌉mu no ni tsu⌈kaima⌉su.** ものを包むのに使います。

Kawa: **Mono,** "a thing" or "things;" **tsutsumu,** "wrap;" "for wrapping,"

Goto: **Tsu⌈tsu⌉mu no ni.** 包むのに

Kawa: **Tsukaimasu,** "to use." "We use it to wrap things in."

Goto: Mo⌐no⌐ o tsu⌐tsu⌐mu no ni tsu⌐kaima⌐su.　ものを包むのに使います。

Kawa: Remember the useful phrase "such and such **ni tsukaimasu,**" "to use for such and such." Let's change a little. "We use it to carry things on."

Goto: Mo⌐no⌐ o ha⌐kobu⌐ no ni tsu⌐kaima⌐su.　ものを運ぶのに使います。

Kawa: **Hakobu** means "carry;" **hakobu no ni,** "in order to carry." Next, "We use it to have meals with."

Goto: Sho⌐kuji o suru⌐ no ni tsu⌐kaima⌐su.　食事をするのに使います。

Kawa: "In order to have meals with."

Goto: Sho⌐kuji o suru⌐ no ni.　食事をするのに

Kawa: "We use it to have meals with."

Goto: Sho⌐kuji o suru⌐ no ni tsu⌐kaima⌐su.　食事をするのに使います。

Kawa: Our third key sentence also deals with **furoshiki.** "It becomes larger when you spread it out."

Goto: Hi⌐rogere⌐ba ⌐o⌐okiku narimasu.　広げれば大きくなります。

Kawa: **Hirogeraba,** meaning "if" or "when you spread it out," is based on **hirogeru,** "spread out." Mark the sound **eba** in **hirogereba.** It denotes the idea of "if" or "when." So, "if you spread it out:"

Goto: Hi⌐rogere⌐ba.　広げれば

Kawa: "It becomes larger."

Goto: ⌐O⌐okiku narimasu.　大きくなります。

Kawa: Let's put them together.

Goto: Hi⌐rogere⌐ba ⌐o⌐okiku narimasu.　広げれば大きくなります。

Kawa: "It's much larger in size when you spread it out." What if you fold it up then? "Fold," **tatamu;** "when you fold it up," **tatameba.** "It becomes much smaller in size."

Goto: Chi⌐isaku narimasu.　小さくなります。

Kawa: "When you fold it up, it becomes much smaller."

Goto: Ta⌐tame⌐ba ⌐chi⌐isaku narimasu.　たためば小さくなります。

Kawa: One more substitution. "It will wear out if you use it."

Goto: Tsu⌐kae⌐ba ⌐wa⌐ruku narimasu.　使えば悪くなります。

Kawa: **Tsukau,** "use;" **tsukaeba,** "if" or "when you use it;" **waruku narimasu,** "to wear out," or, literally, "become worse." Again, "It will wear out if you use it."

Goto: Tsu⌐kae⌐ba ⌐wa⌐ruku narimasu.　使えば悪くなります。

♪ **Station Break** ͏͏

Kawa: Now, in the second half of this session, we'll discuss each dialogue. Listen to their conversation first.

◆ **Today's Conversation**

I: **Su⌐misu-san, ko⌐re, o⌐kusan ni a⌐gete kudasaimase⌐n ka. Fu⌐roshiki de⌐su.**
スミスさん、これ、奥さんにあげて下さいませんか。ふろしきです。

S: **Ko⌐re wa na⌐n ni tsu⌐kau⌐ n desu ka.** これは何に使うんですか。

I: **Hi⌐rogere⌐ba mo⌐no⌐ o tsu⌐tsu⌐mu no ni tsu⌐kaeru⌐ shi, ka⌐be ni kake⌐reba, ka⌐zari ni⌐ mo narimasu.**
広げればものを包むのに使えるし、壁にかければ、飾りにもなります。

S: **A⌐a, so⌐o desu ka. Ta⌐tame⌐ba ⌐chi⌐isaku naru kara ⌐be⌐nri desu ne.**
ああ、そうですか。たためば小さくなるから便利ですね。

Kawa: Next, you'll listen to its English version.

◆ **Same Conversation in English**

I: Would you give this to your wife? It's a furoshiki.

S: What is this used for?

I: You can use it to wrap things in when you spread it out, and you can use it as a decoration if you hang it on the wall.

S: Is that right? It is handy because it becomes small if you fold it up.

Kawa: Now each dialogue. "Mr. Smith, would you give this to Mrs. Smith? It's a furoshiki," Mrs. Ito asks him.

Goto: **Su⌐misu-san, ko⌐re, o⌐kusan ni a⌐gete kudasaimase⌐n ka. Fu⌐roshiki de⌐su.**
スミスさん、これ、奥さんにあげて下さいませんか。ふろしきです。

Kawa: This contains our first key sentence, remember? Her present to Mrs. Smith is a furoshiki. "What is this used for?" Mr. Smith wonders.

Goto: **Ko⌐re wa na⌐n ni tsu⌐kau⌐ n desu ka.** これは何に使うんですか。

Kawa: **Nan ni,** "what for;" **tsukau,** "use." **N desu ka,** in **tsukau n desu ka,** "is it used?" is indicative of personal concern or interest. "What is it used for, I wonder."

Goto: **Ko⌐re wa na⌐n ni tsu⌐kau⌐ n desu ka.** これは何に使うんですか。

Kawa: Mrs. Ito explains. "You can use it to wrap things in when you spread it out, and it becomes a decoration if you hang it on the wall." It contains today's key sentences two and three. Now, we'll deal with it one by one. "When you spread it out:"

Goto: **Hi⌐rogere⌐ba.** 広げれば

Kawa: "You can use it to wrap things in when you spread it out, and...."

Goto: **Hi⌐rogere⌐ba mo⌐no⌐ o tsu⌐tsu⌐mu no ni tsu⌐kaeru⌐ shi,**
広げればものを包むのに使えるし、

Kawa: "if you hang it on the wall…;" "hang," **kakeru**; "wall," **kabe**:

Goto: **Ka⌈be ni kake⌉reba,** 壁にかければ、

Kawa: "it becomes a decoration, too." "Decoration," **kazari**.

Goto: **Ka⌈zari ni⌉ mo narimasu.** 飾りにもなります。

Kawa: "It also becomes a decoration if you hang it on the wall."

Goto: **Ka⌈be ni kake⌉reba, ka⌈zari ni⌉ mo narimasu.**
壁にかければ、飾りにもなります。

Kawa: "Oh, is that so? It is handy because it becomes small if you fold it up," says Mr. Smith.

Goto: **A⌉a, so⌉o desu ka. Ta⌈tame⌉ba ⌈chi⌉isaku ⌈na⌉ru kara ⌈be⌉nri desu ne.**
ああ、そうですか。たためば小さくなるから便利ですね。

Kawa: **Aa** is nearly equal to "oh!" "Oh, is that so?"

Goto: **A⌉a, so⌉o desu ka.** ああ、そうですか。

Kawa: "Because it becomes small if you fold it up."

Goto: **Ta⌈tame⌉ba ⌈chi⌉isaku ⌈na⌉ru kara.** たためば小さくなるから

Kawa: "It is handy, isn't it?"

Goto: **Be⌉nri desu ne.** 便利ですね。

Kawa: The whole sentence again. "Oh, is that so? It is handy because it becomes small if you fold it up."

Goto: **A⌉a, so⌉o desu ka. Ta⌈tame⌉ba ⌈chi⌉isaku ⌈na⌉ru kara ⌈be⌉nri desu ne.**
ああ、そうですか。たためば小さくなるから便利ですね。

Kawa: Let's now listen to the whole conversation again.

◆ **Today's Conversation**

I: **Su⌉misu-san, ko⌈re, o⌉kusan ni a⌈gete kudaimase⌉n ka. Fu⌈roshiki de⌉su.**
スミスさん、これ、奥さんにあげて下さいませんか。ふろしきです。

S: **Ko⌈re wa na⌉n ni tsu⌈kau⌉ n desu ka.** これは何に使うんですか。

I: **Hi⌈rogere⌉ba mo⌈no⌉ o tsu⌈tsu⌉mu no ni tsu⌈kaeru⌉ shi, ka⌈be ni kake⌉reba, ka⌈zari ni⌉ mo narimasu.**
広げればものを包むのに使えるし、壁にかければ、飾りにもなります。

S: **A⌉a, so⌉o desu ka. Ta⌈tame⌉ba ⌈chi⌉isaku naru kara ⌈be⌉nri desu ne.**
ああ、そうですか。たためば小さくなるから便利ですね。

Kawa: Next, as usual, you'll practice today's vocabulary. Please repeat aloud after Goto-san, who will say each word or phrase twice. First, "wrapping cloth."

Goto: **Fu⌈roshiki.** ふろしき

Kawa: "Wall."

Goto: **Ka⌈be.** 壁

Kawa: "Decoration."

Goto: **Ka⌈zari.** 飾り

Kawa: "If" or "when you fold it."

Goto: **Ta⌈tame⌉ba.** たためば

Kawa: Now the key sentences again. This time, just listen to Goto-san. The first key sentence: "Would you give this to your wife?"

Goto: **Ko⌈re, o⌉kusan ni a⌈gete kudasaimase⌉n ka.**
これ、奥さんにあげて下さいませんか。

Kawa: Next, the second key sentence: "It's used for wrapping things in."

Goto: **Mo⌈no⌉ o tsu⌈tsu⌉mu no ni tsu⌈kaima⌉su.** ものを包むのに使います。

Kawa: The third key sentence: "It becomes large when you spread it out."

Goto: **Hi⌈rogere⌉ba ⌈o⌉okiku narimasu.** 広げれば大きくなります。

Kawa: Now, before winding up, you'll listen to their conversation again.

◆ **Today's Conversation**

I: **Su⌉misu-san, ko⌈re, o⌉kusan ni a⌈gete kudasaimase⌉n ka. Fu⌈roshiki de⌉su.**
スミスさん、これ、奥さんにあげて下さいませんか。ふろしきです。

S: **Ko⌈re wa na⌉n ni tsu⌈kau⌉ n desu ka.** これは何に使うんですか。

I: **Hi⌈rogere⌉ba mo⌈no⌉ o tsu⌈tsu⌉mu no ni tsu⌈kaeru⌉ shi, ka⌈be ni kake⌉reba, ka⌈zari ni⌉ mo narimasu.**
ひろげればものを包むのに使えるし、壁にかければ、飾りにもなります。

S: **A⌉a, so⌉o desu ka. Ta⌈tame⌉ba ⌈chi⌉isaku naru kara ⌈be⌉nri desu ne.**
ああ、そうですか。たためば小さくなるから便利ですね。

Notes

1. O⌉kusan ni a⌈gete kudasaimase⌉n ka.

Please learn this pattern thoroughly as a very polite way of making a request.

2. Mo⌈no⌉ o tsu⌈tsu⌉mu no ni tsu⌈kaeru.

You have learned that **no ni** can mean "in spite of the fact that," as in **Ta⌈ka⌉i no ni ka⌈ima⌉shita.** ("He bought it in spite of the fact that it was expensive." Or: "He bought it though it was expensive.") You have also learned **Ko⌈ojo⌉o e ke⌈ngaku ni ikima⌉shita.** ("I went to the factory to observe.") Here, X **ni** indicates the purpose of X. In **Mo⌈no⌉ o tsu⌈tsu⌉mu no ni tsu⌈kau. ni** also signifies "purpose." ("You can use it for wrapping things.")

3. Ta⌐tame⌐ba ⌐chi⌐isaku naru.

For practical purposes, you replace the final -**u** of a verb with -**eba** and the final -**i** of adjectives with -**kereba** to express the idea of "if." With noun + **da**, replace **da** with -**de areba** (or **naraba**).

A⌐me ga fureba, i⌐kimase⌐n. ("I will not go if it rains.")
Ya⌐sukereba, ka⌐ima⌐su. ("I will buy it if it is cheap.")
Byo⌐oki de a⌐reba, i⌐kima⌐sen. ("I will not go if I am ill.")

You have learned the expression "have to" or "must" as it occurs in sentences like: **I⌐kana⌐kereba narimasen.** ("It will not do if I don't go." i.e., "I must go.") Here, too, the -**eba** form is used. The clause with -**eba** indicates the condition that will definitely bring about the resultant state or action described in the phrase that follows. So, **Ya⌐sukereba ka⌐ima⌐su** means "I will definitely buy it, if it is cheap." This sentence, however, also implies: "If it is not cheap, I will not buy it."

Additional Vocabulary

fu⌐de	(筆)	brush (for writing or painting)
ji⌐ o ⌐ka⌐ku	(字を書く)	to write characters
mo⌐no⌐ o ha⌐kobu	(物を運ぶ)	to carry things
me⌐gane	(めがね)	eyeglasses
me⌐gane o ka⌐ke⌐ru	(めがねを掛ける)	to put on eyeglasses

Exercises

1. Using -**te ku⌐dasaimase⌐n ka**, change the cue into a polite request.

Example: **tsu⌐kau→Ko⌐re, tsu⌐katte kudasaimase⌐n ka.**

1. **Mo⌐tte iku.**
2. **O⌐kusan ni a⌐geru.**
3. **Go⌐shu⌐jin ni a⌐geru.**
4. **Fu⌐de de ka⌐ku.**
5. **Tsu⌐katte mi⌐ru.**

2. Making necessary changes, add **no ni tsu⌐kaima⌐su** to each of the following sentences.

Example: **Mo⌐no⌐ o tsu⌐tsumima⌐su.→Mo⌐no⌐ o tsu⌐tsu⌐mu no ni tsu⌐kaima⌐su.**

1. **Sho⌐kuji o shima⌐su.**
2. **J⌐i o ka⌐kima⌐su.**
3. **Shi⌐nbun o yomima⌐su.**
4. **Mo⌐no⌐ o ha⌐kobima⌐su.**
5. **De⌐nwa o kakema⌐su.**
6. **Se⌐ehin no tsukurika⌐ta o se⌐tsumee shima⌐su.**
7. **Ryo⌐koo no hanashi⌐ o shimasu.**

3. Substitute the cue for the underlined word in the model sentence.

Model Sentence: <u>Fu⌐roshiki</u> wa na⌐ni ni tsukau n desu ka.

1. ha⌐shi
2. fu⌐de
3. me⌐gane
4. ku⌐ruma
5. ko⌐no ka⌐ado
6. ko⌐no shashin
7. ko⌐no chi⌐zu

4. Practice dialogues between A and B. For person A, use the sentences formed in Exercise 3. For person B, use the sentences formed in Exercise 2.

Model Dialogue: A: Fu⌐roshiki wa na⌐ni ni tsukau n desu ka.
                 B: Mo⌐no⌐ o tsu⌐tsu⌐mu no ni tsukaimasu.

5. Give the -eba form of the following verbs.

1. i⌐ku
2. yo⌐mu
3. ta⌐tamu
4. hi⌐rogeru
5. a⌐u
6. tsu⌐kau
7. ki⌐ku
8. ka⌐ke⌐ru
9. su⌐ru
10. ku⌐ru
11. ta⌐ka⌐i
12. i⌐i (or yo⌐i)
13. na⌐i
14. no⌐ma⌐nai
15. o⌐oi

6. Using the -eba form, combine the two parts of each cue.

Example: hi⌐rogeru; o⌐oki⌐ku naru→Hi⌐rogere⌐ba o⌐okiku narimasu.

1. ta⌐tamu; chi⌐isaku naru
2. ko⌐oban de michi o kiku; wa⌐ka⌐ru
3. ta⌐ka⌐i; ka⌐ita⌐ku ⌐na⌐i
4. me⌐gane o ka⌐ke⌐nai; yo⌐me⌐nai
5. ma⌐inichi re⌐nshuu shina⌐i; de⌐ki⌐nai

7. Give B's part, changing the cue sentence into an -**eba** clause.

Example: (**tatamu**)

A: Chi⌐isaku narimasu ka.

B: E⌐e, <u>ta⌐tame⌐ba</u>, chi⌐isaku narimasu yo.

1. A: Mi⌐chi ga wakarima⌐su ka.
   B: (ko⌐oban de kiku)

2. A: Ka⌐ima⌐su ka.
   B: (ne⌐dan ga yasu⌐i)

3. A: Ha⌐yaku ha⌐shire⌐ru yoo ni na⌐rima⌐su ka.
   B: (ma⌐inichi re⌐nshuu suru)

4. A: Fu⌐ji-san ga mi⌐ema⌐su ka.
   B: (Te⌐nki ga ⌐i⌐i)

5. A: O⌐okiku narimasu ka.
   B: (hi⌐rogeru)

Answers

1. 1. Ko⌐re, mo⌐tte i⌐tte kudasaimasen ka.
   2. Ko⌐re, o⌐kusan ni a⌐gete kudasaimase⌐n ka.
   3. Ko⌐re, go⌐shu⌐jin ni a⌐gete kudasaimase⌐n ka.
   4. Ko⌐re, fu⌐de de ka⌐ite kudasaimasen ka.
   5. Ko⌐re, tsu⌐katte mi⌐te kudasaimasen ka.

2. 1. Sho⌐kuji o suru⌐ no ni tsukaimasu.
   2. Ji⌐ o kaku no ni tsu⌐kaima⌐su.
   3. Shi⌐nbun o yo⌐mu no ni tsu⌐kaima⌐su.
   4. Mo⌐no⌐ o ha⌐kobu⌐ no ni tsukaimasu.
   5. De⌐nwa o kake⌐ru no ni tsukaimasu.
   6. Se⌐ehin no tsukurikata⌐ o se⌐tsumee suru⌐ no ni tsukaimasu.
   7. Ryo⌐koo no hanashi⌐ o su⌐ru⌐ no ni tsukaimasu.

3. 1. Ha⌐shi wa ⌐na⌐ni ni tsu⌐kau⌐ n desu ka.
   2. Fu⌐de wa na⌐ni ni tsu⌐kau⌐ n desu ka.
   3. Me⌐gane wa ⌐na⌐ni ni tsu⌐kau⌐ n desu ka.
   4. Ku⌐ruma wa na⌐ni ni tsu⌐kau⌐ n desu ka.
   5. Ko⌐no ka⌐ado wa ⌐na⌐ni ni tsu⌐kau⌐ n desu ka.
   6. Ko⌐no shashin wa na⌐ni ni tsu⌐kau⌐ n desu ka.
   7. Ko⌐no chi⌐zu wa ⌐na⌐ni ni tsu⌐kau⌐ n desu ka.

5. 1. i⌐ke⌐ba
   2. yo⌐meba
   3. ta⌐tame⌐ba
   4. hi⌐rogere⌐ba
   5. a⌐eba
   6. tsu⌐kae⌐ba
   7. ki⌐ke⌐ba
   8. ka⌐ke⌐reba

9. su⌈re⌋ba
10. ku⌋reba
11. ta⌋kakereba
12. yo⌋kereba (always **yo⌋kereba**, never **i⌋kereba**)
13. na⌋kereba
14. no⌈ma⌋nakereba
15. o⌋okereba

6. 1. Ta⌈tame⌋ba ⌈chi⌋isaku narimasu.
   2. Ko⌈oban de kike⌋ba wa⌈karima⌋su
   3. Ta⌋kakereba ka⌈itaku arimase⌋n.
   4. Me⌋gane o ka⌈ke⌋nakereba yo⌈memase⌋n.
   5. Ma⌋inichi re⌈nshuu shina⌋kereba de⌈kimase⌋n.

7. 1. B: Ko⌈oban de kike⌋ba wa⌈karima⌋su yo.
   2. B: Ne⌈dan ga ya⌋sukereba ka⌈ima⌋su.
   3. B: Ma⌋inichi re⌈nshuu sure⌋ba ⌈ha⌋yaku ha⌈shire⌋ru yoo ni na⌈rima⌋su yo.
   4. B: Te⌋nki ga ⌈yo⌋kereba ⌈Fu⌋ji-san ga mi⌈ema⌋su yo.
   5. B: Hi⌈rogere⌋ba ⌈o⌋okiku narimasu yo.

I⌐TOO⌐-KE DE O⌐WAKARE NO KA⌐I
伊藤家でお別れの会（続き）
Farewell Party at the Itos' - continued

Today's Conversation

Smith: **I⌐roiro⌐ o⌐se⌐wa ni na⌐rima⌐shita.**
いろいろお世話になりました。
Thank you very much for your kindness to me.

Ito: **I⌐ie, na⌐ni mo⌐ de⌐kimase⌐n deshita kedo.**
いいえ、何もできませんでしたけど。
Not at all. We couldn't do much for you.

Smith: **O⌐kagesama de⌐ byo⌐oki mo ji⌐ko mo naku, ke⌐ngaku ya ryokoo mo de⌐kite, ho⌐ntoo ni yo⌐katta desu.**
おかげさまで病気も事故もなく、見学や旅行もできて、ほんとうによかったです。
Thanks to you, I had a wonderful time observing and traveling, without becoming sick or meeting any accident.

Ito: **De⌐mo, mo⌐o o⌐wakare na⌐nte, za⌐nne⌐n desu ne.**
でも、もうお別れなんて、残念ですね。
It's a pity, isn't it, to have to say good-bye now.

Smith: **Wa⌐tashi mo⌐ mo⌐o suko⌐shi i⌐ta⌐i n desu ga, a⌐mari kaeri⌐ ga o⌐soku na⌐ru to ku⌐bi ni na⌐tte shi⌐maima⌐su kara.**
私ももう少しいたいんですが、あまり帰りが遅くなるとクビになってしまいますから。
I would very much like to stay longer, but if I don't return soon, I will be fired.

Ito: **Ko¹ndo wa ⌈o¹kusan ya ko⌈domo-san o tsurete¹ kite kudasai ⌈ne.**

こんどは奥さんや子供さんをつれてきて下さいね。

Please bring your wife and children when you come next time.

ITOO-KE DE OWAKARE NO KAI
伊藤家でお別れの会（続き）
Farewell Party - continued

Kawa: Today, in Lesson 51, the Itos are still having a farewell party for Mr. Smith. He thanks Mrs. Ito for having been so kind to him. Mrs. Ito is sorry he'll have to leave Japan pretty soon. Our first key sentence is, "It's a pity, isn't it, to have to part now."

Goto: **Mo¹o o⌈wakare na¹nte, za⌈nne¹n desu ne.**
もうお別れなんて、残念ですね。

Kawa: **Moo**, "already;" **owakare**, "parting;" **zannen desu**, "it is a pity." **Nante** in **owakare nante** denotes emotional connotations used mostly in spoken Japanese. "It's a pity really to have to part now."

Goto: **Mo¹o o⌈wakare na¹nte, za⌈nne¹n desu ne.**
もうお別れなんて、残念ですね。

Kawa: Let's change a bit. "It's a pity, really, you have to leave so soon."

Goto: **Mo¹o o⌈kaeri na¹nte, za⌈nne¹n desu ne.**
もうお帰りなんて、残念ですね。

Kawa: **Okaeri**, "your returning home." Listen again.

Goto: **Mo¹o o⌈kaeri na¹nte, za⌈nne¹n desu ne.**
もうお帰りなんて、残念ですね。

Kawa: Our second key sentence deals with **to**, which indicates the cause and effect of things, as in "If I delay my return too much, the president will give me a good scolding."

Goto: **O⌈soku na¹ru to, sha⌈choo ni¹ shi⌈karare¹masu.**
遅くなると、社長に叱られます。

Kawa: **Osoku naru to** literally means "if it becomes late;" **shachoo**, "the president of a company;" **shikararemasu**, "to be scolded" or "given a good talking-to." "The president will scold me unless I return soon."

Goto: **O⌈soku na¹ru to, sha⌈choo ni¹ shi⌈karare¹masu.**
遅くなると、社長に叱られます。

Kawa: Let's change a bit. "My wife will start worrying if I don't return soon."

Goto: Oˈsoku naˈru to, kaˈnai ga shiˈnpai shimaˈsu.
遅くなると、家内が心配します。

Kawa: **Kanai** means "my wife;" **shinpai shimasu**, "to worry." "Unless I go home early enough, my wife will worry about me."

Goto: Oˈsoku naˈru to, kaˈnai ga shiˈnpai shimaˈsu.
遅くなると、家内が心配します。

♪ **Station Break** ⅲⅲⅲ

Kawa: In the second half of this program, we'll discuss each dialogue as usual. Listen to the whole conversation first.

◆ **Today's Conversation**

S: Iˈroiroˈ oˈseˈwa ni naˈrimaˈshita. いろいろお世話になりました。

I: Iˈie, naˈni moˈ deˈkimaseˈn deshita kedo.
いいえ、何もできませんでしたけど。

S: Oˈkagesama deˈ byoˈoki mo jiˈko mo naku, keˈngaku ya ryokoo mo deˈkite, hoˈntoo ni yoˈkatta desu.
おかげさまで病気も事故もなく、見学や旅行もできて、ほんとうによかったです。

I: Deˈmo, moˈo oˈwakare naˈnte, zaˈnneˈn desu ne.
でも、もうお別れなんて、残念ですね。

S: Waˈtashi moˈ moˈo sukoˈshi iˈtaˈi n desu ga, aˈmari kaeriˈ ga oˈsoku naˈru to kuˈbi ni naˈtte shiˈmaimaˈsu kara.
私ももう少しいたいんですが、あまり帰りが遅くなるとクビになってしまいますから。

I: Koˈndo wa ˈoˈkusan ya koˈdomo-san o tsureteˈ kite kudasai ˈne.
こんどは奥さんや子供さんをつれてきて下さいね。

Kawa: Next, you'll listen to its English version.

◆ **Same Conversation in English**

S: Thank you very much for your kindness to me.

I: Not at all. We couldn't do much for you.

S: Thanks to you, I had a wonderful time observing and traveling, without becoming sick or meeting any accident.

I: It's a pity, isn't it, to have to say good-bye now.

S: I would very much like to stay longer, but if I don't return soon, I will be fired.

I: Please bring your wife and children when you come next time.

Kawa: Now, each dialogue. Mr. Smith is very grateful to Mr. and Mrs. Ito. "Thank you very much for your kindness to me."

Goto: I⌈roiro⌉ o⌈se⌉wa ni na⌈rima⌉shita.　いろいろお世話になりました。

Kawa: **Iroiro** means "in various ways" or "for many things" in the context. **Osewa ni narimashita** is an idiomatic expression for "Thank you very much for your kindness." Just remember the sentence. Listen again.

Goto: I⌈roiro⌉ o⌈se⌉wa ni na⌈rima⌉shita.　いろいろお世話になりました。

Kawa: "Not at all," responds Mrs. Ito. "We couldn't do much for you."

Goto: I⌈ie, na⌈ni mo⌉ de⌈kimase⌉n deshita kedo.
いいえ、何もできませんでしたけど。

Kawa: **Nani mo**, "anything" used in negative context; **dekimasen deshita**, "couldn't do." **Kedo** itself, meaning "although," only helps to soften the expression. "Not at all. We couldn't do much for you, I'm afraid."

Goto: I⌈ie, na⌈ni mo⌉ de⌈kimase⌉n deshita kedo.
いいえ、何もできませんでしたけど。

Kawa: This is one of the common ways of greeting. Just remember the expression. In Japan, Mr. Smith said, he had a wonderful time observing and traveling, without becoming sick or meeting any accident. We follow his expressions one by one. He starts his remark with "Thanks to you...."

Goto: O⌈kagesama de⌉　おかげさまで、

Kawa: It's a set phrase for "Thanks to you." "I had a wonderful time."

Goto: Ho⌈ntoo ni yo⌉katta desu.　ほんとうによかったです。

Kawa: This literally reads, "It was truly good." "Observing and traveling."

Goto: Ke⌈ngaku ya ryokoo mo de⌉kite.　見学や旅行もできて、

Kawa: **Kengaku**, "observing;" **ryokoo**, "traveling;" **dekite**, "we were able to do something, and...." Next, "without becoming sick or meeting any accident."

Goto: Byo⌈oki mo ji⌉ko mo ⌈na⌉ku.　病気も事故もなく、

Kawa: **Byooki**, "sickness;" **jiko**, "accident;" **naku**, "there was none, and...." You'll now listen to the entire remark. "Thanks to you, I had a wonderful time observing and traveling, without becoming sick or meeting any accident."

Goto: O⌈kagesama de⌉ byo⌈oki mo ji⌉ko mo ⌈na⌉ku, ke⌈ngaku ya⌉ ryo⌈koo⌉ mo de⌈kite, ho⌈ntoo ni yo⌉katta desu.
おかげさまで病気も事故もなく、見学や旅行もできて、ほんとうによかったです。

Kawa: Next, we hear the first key sentence, the remark made by Mrs. Ito. "It's a pity, isn't it, to have to part now."

Goto: De⌐mo, mo⌐o o⌐wakare na⌐nte, za⌐nne⌐n desu ne.
　　　　でも、もうお別れなんて、残念ですね。

Kawa: Mr. Smith doesn't want to leave either. But he must. He says, "I would very much like to stay longer, but if I delay my return too much, I'll get the sack."

Goto: Wa⌐tashi mo⌐ mo⌐o suko⌐shi i⌐ta⌐i n desu ga, a⌐mari kaeri⌐ ga o⌐soku na⌐ru to ku⌐bi ni na⌐tte shi⌐maima⌐su kara.
　　　　私ももう少しいたいんですが、あまり帰りが遅くなるとクビになってしまいますから。

Kawa: **Watashi mo moo sukoshi itai n desu ga,** "I also would like to stay a little longer, if I could." Listen again.

Goto: **Wa⌐tashi mo⌐ mo⌐o suko⌐shi i⌐ta⌐i n desu ga,**
　　　　私ももう少しいたいんですが、

Kawa: "If I delay my return too much, I'll get the sack."

Goto: **A⌐mari kaeri⌐ ga o⌐soku na⌐ru to ku⌐bi ni na⌐tte shi⌐maima⌐su kara.**
　　　　あまり帰りが遅くなるとクビになってしまいますから。

Kawa: **Amari,** "too much;" **kaeri,** "my return home;" **kubi ni natte shimaimasu,** "to get the sack." It's a colloquial expression meaning literally "to get the head cut off," in other words, "discharged." Mrs. Ito would like him to bring his wife and children when he comes next time.

Goto: **Ko⌐ndo wa ⌐o⌐kusan ya ko⌐domo-san o tsurete⌐ kite kudasai ne.**
　　　　こんどは奥さんや子供さんをつれてきて下さいね。

Kawa: **Kondo wa,** "next time;" **kodomo-san,** "your children;" **tsurete kite kudasai,** "please bring here." "Please bring your wife and children when you come next time."

Goto: **Ko⌐ndo wa ⌐o⌐kusan ya ko⌐domo-san o tsurete⌐ kite kudasai ne.**
　　　　こんどは奥さんや子供さんをつれてきて下さいね。

Kawa: Now you'll listen to the whole conversation again.

◆ **Today's Conversation**

S: **I⌐roiro⌐ o⌐se⌐wa ni na⌐rima⌐shita.** いろいろお世話になりました。

I: **I⌐ie, na⌐ni mo⌐ de⌐kimase⌐n deshita kedo.**
　　いいえ、何もできませんでしたけど。

S: **O⌐kagesama de⌐ byo⌐oki mo ji⌐ko mo naku, ke⌐ngaku ya ryokoo mo de⌐kite, ho⌐ntoo ni yo⌐katta desu.**
　　おかげさまで病気も事故もなく、見学や旅行もできて、ほんとうによかったです。

I: **De⌐mo, mo⌐o o⌐wakare na⌐nte, za⌐nne⌐n desu ne.**
　　でも、もうお別れなんて、残念ですね。

S: **Wa⌐tashi mo⌐ mo⌐o suko⌐shi i⌐ta⌐i n desu ga, a⌐mari kaeri⌐ ga o⌐soku na⌐ru to ku⌐bi ni na⌐tte shi⌐maima⌐su kara.**
私ももう少しいたいんですが、あまり帰りが遅くなるとクビになってしまいますから。

I: **Ko⌐ndo wa ⌐o⌐kusan ya ko⌐domo-san o tsurete⌐ kite kudasai ⌐ne.**
こんどは奥さんや子供さんをつれてきて下さいね。

Kawa: You'll now review today's vocabulary. Please repeat aloud after Goto-san, who'll say each word or phrase twice. First, "sickness."

Goto: **Byo⌐oki.** 病気

Kawa: "Accident."

Goto: **Ji⌐ko.** 事故

Kawa: "Parting."

Goto: **O⌐wakare.** お別れ

Kawa: "Get the sack;" "be fired."

Goto: **Ku⌐bi ni na⌐ru.** クビになる

Kawa: Now, today's key sentences. This time, just listen to Goto-san. Today's first key sentence: "it's a pity, isn't it, to have to part now."

Goto: **Mo⌐o o⌐wakare na⌐nte, za⌐nne⌐n desu ne.**
もうお別れなんて、残念ですね。

Kawa: The second key sentence: "The president [boss] will give me a good scolding if I delay my return too much."

Goto: **O⌐soku na⌐ru to, sha⌐choo ni⌐ shi⌐karare⌐masu.**
遅くなると、社長に叱られます。

Kawa: Now, before we wind up, let's listen to the whole dialogue again.

◆ **Today's Conversation**

S: **I⌐roiro⌐ o⌐se⌐wa ni na⌐rima⌐shita.** いろいろお世話になりました。

I: **I⌐ie, na⌐ni mo⌐ de⌐kimase⌐n deshita kedo.**
いいえ、何もできませんでしたけど。

S: **O⌐kagesama de⌐ byo⌐oki mo ji⌐ko mo naku, ke⌐ngaku ya ryokoo mo de⌐kite, ho⌐ntoo ni yo⌐katta desu.**
おかげさまで病気も事故もなく、見学や旅行もできて、ほんとうによかったです。

I: **De⌐mo, mo⌐o o⌐wakare na⌐nte, za⌐nne⌐n desu ne.**
でも、もうお別れなんて、残念ですね。

S: **Wa⌐tashi mo⌐ mo⌐o suko⌐shi i⌐ta⌐i n desu ga, a⌐mari kaeri⌐ ga o⌐soku na⌐ru to ku⌐bi ni na⌐tte shi⌐maima⌐su kara.**
私ももう少しいたいんですが、あまり帰りが遅くなるとクビになってしまいますから。

I: Ko⌐ndo wa ⌐o⌐kusan ya ko⌐domo-san o tsurete⌐ kite kudasai ⌐ne.
こんどは奥さんや子供さんをつれてきて下さいね。

Notes

1. I⌐roiro⌐ o⌐se⌐wa ni narimashita.

When you leave someone's home or office and want to thank your host for his or her hospitality or trouble, say **Do⌐omo a⌐ri⌐gatoo gozaimashita.** and **I⌐roiro⌐ o⌐se⌐wa ni narimashita.** Your host will answer with **Na⌐ni mo dekimase⌐n deshita** ("I could not do anything [special]") or **Na⌐ni mo oyaku ni tachimase⌐n de.** ("I wasn't able to be of any [special] help").

O⌐se⌐wa ni naru is an expression you will hear very often in Japan. **I⌐tsumo o⌐se⌐wa ni natte orimasu** (o⌐rima⌐su is the humble equivalent of i⌐ma⌐su) will be said by a wife to her husband's friends or superiors, by a mother to her child's teacher and to other mothers, by a company's telephone operator to its customers, clients, or even to its competitors as a formal greeting. **I⌐ie, ko⌐chira ko⌐so o⌐se⌐wa ni ⌐na⌐tte orimasu** (literally, "No, it is I who have been receiving your kind help") is a likely response.

2. O⌐soku na⌐ru to, ku⌐bi ni na⌐ru.

Present tense verbs and adjectives come before **to** when it is used to connect two clauses in a cause and effect relationship, as in "If A happens, B will follow." "Whenever A happens B will occur as a matter of course."

Shi⌐gatu⌐ ni naru to sa⌐kura ga sakima⌐su. ("When April comes, cherry blossoms bloom.")

A⌐mari yasu⌐i to mi⌐nna kaitaku narima⌐su ne. ("If things are so cheap, we want to buy everything, don't we?")

A⌐sa o⌐ki⌐ru to ⌐su⌐gu ko⌐ohi⌐i o no⌐mima⌐su. Yo⌐ru wa no⌐mimase⌐n. Yo⌐ru ⌐no⌐mu to ne⌐rarenaku na⌐ru n desu. ("I drink coffee as soon as I get up in the morning. I don't drink it in the evening. If I drink it in the evening, I won't be able to get to sleep.")

Exercises

1. Substitute the cues for the underlined portions of the model sentence.

Model Sentence: <u>Mo⌐o o⌐wakare</u> na⌐nte <u>za⌐nne⌐n</u> desu ne.

1. mo⌐o ka⌐eru; za⌐nne⌐n
2. mo⌐o o⌐wari; sa⌐bishi⌐i
3. ju⌐uman-en; ta⌐ka⌐i
4. ha⌐tachi; wa⌐ka⌐i
5. byo⌐oki ni na⌐ru; za⌐nne⌐n
6. shi⌐ai ni makeru; za⌐nne⌐n
7. ryo⌐koo ni ikeru; u⌐reshi⌐i

8. mo˺o o˹wakare; sa˹bishi˺i
9. Ni˹hongo mo Furansugo mo hanase˺ru; i˹i
10. Yo˹shiko-san ga ke˹kkon suru; u˹reshi˺i

2. Substitute the cue for the underlined phrase in the model sentence.

Model Sentence: O˹soku na˺ru to <u>sha˹choo ni shikarareru˺</u> n desu yo.

1. ka˺nai ga shi˹npai suru
2. shu˺jin ga shi˹npai suru
3. ha˺ha ga shi˹npai suru
4. de˹nsha ga˺ na˹ku naru
5. mi˹nna˺ ga ko˹ma˺ru
6. ta˺kushii ga su˹kuna˺ku ˹na˺ru
7. mi˹chi ga ko˺mu
8. o˹naka ga suku
9. mi˹se˺ ga mi˹nna shima˺tte shimau
10. sa˺muku naru

3. Substitute the cue for the underlined phrase in the model sentence.

Model Sentence: <u>Byo˹oki ni na˺ru</u> to ko˹marima˺su kara, ki ˹o tsuke˺te imasu.

1. o˹kureru
2. ji˹ko ni ˹a˺u
3. o˹kane o torare˺ru
4. a˹shi˺ o fu˹mareru
5. fu˹to˺ru
6. o˹kane o tsukaisugi˺ru
7. chi˹chi˺ ni shi˹karareru
8. tsu˹karesugi˺ru
9. me˺ ga ˹wa˺ruku naru
10. do˹roboo ni hairare˺ru

4. The following conversation takes place between Mr. A, who came to Japan to learn about plant management, and Mr. B, a plant manager. B has spent 3 days showing his plant to A, who is now leaving. Please choose words or phrases from the list given below to fill in the blanks.

A: B-san, do˺omo a˹ri˺gatoo go˹zaima˺shita. I˹roiro (1)[   ] narima˺shita.
B: I˹ie, (2)[   ] de˹kimase˺n deshita kedo.
A: (3)[   ] ro˹bo˺tto no koto (4)[   ], se˹ehin ke˺nsa no koto nado, i˹roiro wakarima˺shita.
B: Mo˺o o˹kaeri (5)[   ], za˹nne˺n desu ne.
A: E˺e, mo˺tto i˹ta˺i n desu ga, shi˹goto ga ma˺tte imasu (6)[   ].
B: So˺o desu ka. Ma˺ta kite˺ kudasai.

A: Aˈriˈgatoo gozaimasu. Ja, (7)[   ] shimasu.
B: (8)[   ] oˈkaeri kudasai.

(a) ya
(b) ki ˈo tsukeˈte
(c) shiˈtsuˈree
(d) toˈ iˈtteˈ mo
(e) naˈnte
(f) saˈbishiˈi

(g) oˈseˈwa ni
(h) oˈkagesama de
(i) to
(j) kaˈra
(k) naˈni mo

5. Ms. Takada has just returned to the office from vacation. She is now talking with Mr. Sato, who joined the company only recently. Please fill in the blanks in their conversation with words selected from the list given below.

T: Saˈtoo-san, koˈre, oˈmiyage deˈsu.
S: E? Oˈmiyage naˈnte (1)[   ] desu ne. Naˈn desu ka.
T: Neˈkutai desu. Iˈroˈ ga aˈkarusugimaˈsu ka.
S: (2)[   ], kiˈree (3)[   ] iˈroˈ desu yo.
T: Aˈoˈi ˈsuˈutsu ni koˈno neˈkutai o (4)[   ] to iˈi (5)[   ] oˈmoimaˈsu (6)[   ]....
S: Soˈo desu ne. A, yuˈnyuuhin deˈsu ne.
T: Eˈe, (7)[   ] Niˈppon no iroˈ to ˈchoˈtto (8)[   ] deshoo?
S: Aˈshita, daˈigaku no tokiˈ no tomodachi (9)[   ] aˈu (10)[   ], koˈre shiˈmete (11)[   ]. Doˈomo aˈriˈgatoo gozaimashita.
T: Iˈie.

(a) iˈie
(b) haˈi
(c) uˈreshiˈi
(d) daˈ kara
(e) ni
(f) keˈdo
(g) zaˈnneˈn
(h) chiˈgau

(i) oˈnaji
(j) iˈkimaˈsu
(k) na
(l) shiˈmeˈru
(m) no
(n) to
(o) noˈde

Answers

1. 1. Moˈo ˈkaˈeru nante zaˈnneˈn desu ne.
   2. Moˈo oˈwari naˈnte saˈbishiˈi desu ne.
   3. Juˈuman-en naˈnte taˈkaˈi desu ne.
   4. Haˈtachi nante waˈkaˈi desu ne.
   5. Byoˈoki ni naˈru nante zaˈnneˈn desu ne.
   6. Shiˈai ni makeruˈ nante zaˈnneˈn desu ne.
   7. Ryoˈkoo ni ikeruˈ nante uˈreshiˈi desu ne.
   8. Moˈo oˈwakareˈ nante saˈbishiˈi desu ne.
   9. Niˈhongo mo Furansugo mo hanaseˈru nante ˈiˈi desu ne.
   10. Yoˈshiko-san ga keˈkkon suruˈ nante uˈreshiˈi desu ne.

2. 1. Oˈsoku naˈru to ˈkaˈnai ga shiˈnpai suruˈ n desu yo.

   2. Oˈsoku naˈru to ˈshuˈjin ga shiˈnpai suruˈ n desu yo.

   3. Oˈsoku naˈru to ˈhaˈha ga shiˈnpai suruˈ n desu yo.

   4. Oˈsoku naˈru to deˈnsha ga naku naruˈ n desu yo.

   5. Oˈsoku naˈru to miˈnnaˈ ga koˈmaˈru n desu yo.

   6. Oˈsoku naˈru to ˈtaˈkushii ga suˈkunaˈkunaru n desu yo.

   7. Oˈsoku naˈru to miˈchi ga koˈmu n desu yo.

   8. Oˈsoku naˈru to oˈnaka ga sukuˈ n desu yo.

   9. Oˈsoku naˈru to miˈseˈ ga miˈnna shimaˈtte shimau n desu yo.

   10. Oˈsoku naˈru to ˈsaˈmuku naru n desu yo.

3. 1. Oˈkureruˈ to koˈmarimaˈsu kara, ki ˈo tsukeˈte imasu.

   2. Jiˈko ni au to koˈmarimaˈsu kara, ki ˈo tsukeˈte imasu.

   3. Oˈkane o torareˈru to koˈmarimaˈsu kara, ki ˈo tsukeˈte imasu.

   4. Aˈshiˈ o fumareru to koˈmarimaˈsu kara, ki ˈo tsukeˈte imasu.

   5. Fuˈtoˈru to koˈmarimaˈsu kara, ki ˈo tsukeˈte imasu.

   6. Oˈkane o tsukaisugiˈru to koˈmarimaˈsu kara, ki ˈo tsukeˈte imasu.

   7. Chiˈchiˈ ni shiˈkarareru to koˈmarimaˈsu kara, ki ˈo tsukeˈte imasu.

   8. Tsuˈkaresugiˈru to koˈmarimaˈsu kara, ki ˈo tsukeˈte imasu.

   9. Meˈ ga ˈwaˈruku naru to koˈmarimaˈsu kara, ki ˈo tsukeˈte imasu.

   10. Doˈroboo ni hairareˈru to koˈmarimaˈsu kara, ki ˈo tsukeˈte imasu.

4. 1. (g)

   2. (k)

   3. (h)

   4. (a)

   5. (e)

   6. (j)

   7. (c)

   8. (b)

5. 1. (c)

   2. (a)

   3. (k)

   4. (l)

   5. (n)

   6. (f)

   7. (d)

   8. (h)

   9. (e)

   10. (o)

   11. (j)

Iᴸᴛᴏᴏᴸ-KE DE Oᴸᴡᴀᴋᴀʀᴇ NO KAᴸɪ
伊藤家でお別れの会（続き）
Farewell Party at the Itos' - continued

Today's Conversation

Smith: **Niᴸppoᴸn ni iᴸru aida niᴸ hiᴸtoᴸtsu uᴸtaᴸ o oᴸboemaᴸshita.**
日本にいる間にひとつ歌をおぼえました。
I learned a song during my stay in Japan.

Ito: **Zeᴸhi uᴸtatte kudasaᴸi.**
ぜひ歌って下さい。
Sing it for us, please.

Smith: **Miᴸnaᴸ-san mo goᴸzoᴸnji no uᴸtaᴸ desu kara, iᴸssho ni utatte kudasaᴸi.**
みなさんもご存じの歌ですから、いっしょに歌って
下さい。
This is a song you all know, so please sing along with me.

Ito: **Soᴸo shimashoᴸo. Kiᴸnen niᴸ roᴸkuon shite okimashoᴸo.**
そうしましょう。記念に録音しておきましょう。
We will do that. I will record it as a reminder of today.

ITOO-KE DE OWAKARE NO KAI

伊藤家でお別れの会（続き）

Farewell Party at the Itos'- continued

Kawa: Today, in Lesson 52, the last in this series, Mr. Smith offers to sing a song he learned in Japan at his farewell party held at the Itos. He says, "I learned various songs during my stay in Japan." This is our first key sentence.

Goto: **Ni⌈ppo⌉n ni i⌈ru aida ni⌉ i⌈roiro⌉ u⌈ta⌉ o o⌈boema⌉shita.**
日本にいる間に、いろいろ歌をおぼえました。

Kawa: **Aida ni** means "during" or "while." **Iru** means "stay," "exist," or "be." So,

Goto: **Ni⌈ppo⌉n ni i⌈ru aida ni.** 日本にいる間に、

Kawa: means "during my stay in Japan," or "while I've stayed in Japan."

Goto: **I⌈roiro** いろいろ

Kawa: means "in various ways;" "in many ways."

Goto: **O⌈boema⌉shita.** おぼえました。

Kawa: "Memorized," which comes from **oboemasu**, "to memorize." **Uta**, "a song" or "songs."

Goto: **U⌈ta⌉ o o⌈boema⌉shita.** 歌をおぼえました。

Kawa: "I've learned songs." Now, the whole sentence: "I've learned many kinds of songs during my stay in Japan."

Goto: **Ni⌈ppo⌉n ni i⌈ru aida ni⌉ i⌈roiro uta⌉ o o⌈boema⌉shita.**
日本にいる間に、いろいろ歌をおぼえました。

Kawa: Next, we'll change the key sentence slightly. Suppose you've learned many words. "Words," **kotoba**. "I've learned many words during my stay in Japan."

Goto: **Ni⌈ppo⌉n ni i⌈ru aida ni⌉ i⌈roiro kotoba⌉ o o⌈boema⌉shita.**
日本にいる間に、いろいろ言葉をおぼえました。

Kawa: Then, how about "I've seen many places during my stay in Japan."

Goto: **Ni⌈ppo⌉n ni i⌈ru aida ni⌉ i⌈roiro na tokoro⌉ o mi⌈ma⌉shita.**
日本にいる間に、いろいろなところを見ました。

Kawa: The phrase for "many" or "various places" is:

Goto: **I⌈roiro na tokoro⌉.** いろいろなところ

Kawa: "Saw," as in "I saw many places," is **mimashita**. The whole sentence again:

Goto: **Ni⌈ppo⌉n ni i⌈ru aida ni⌉ i⌈roiro na tokoro⌉ o mi⌈ma⌉shita.**
日本にいる間に、いろいろなところを見ました。

Kawa: Another substitution. "You've met different kinds of people while you've stayed in Japan."

Goto: **Ni⌈ppo⌉n ni i⌈ru aida ni⌉, i⌈roiro na hito⌉ ni a⌈ima⌉shita.**
日本にいる間に、いろいろな人に会いました。

Kawa: "Met," **aimashita.** "You've met different kinds of people."

Goto: **I⌈roiro na hito⌉ ni a⌈ima⌉shita.** いろいろな人に会いました。

Kawa: Now, back to Mr. Smith, who would like to sing a Japanese song he's learned in this country. It'll be a memorable occasion for them all. Mr. Ito would like to record it. "To record," **rokuon shimasu.** Mr. Ito says, "I will record it." It's our second key sentence.

Goto: **Ro⌈kuon shite okimasho⌉o.** 録音しておきましょう。

Kawa: You've noticed it wasn't **rokuon shimashoo**, which is neutral in meaning, but...

Goto: **Ro⌈kuon shite okimasho⌉o.** 録音しておきましょう。

Kawa: The whole idea is that you'll record it ready for future reference, or as a reminder of the day, or to be prepared for any possible need that may arise in the future.

Goto: **Ro⌈kuon shite okimasho⌉o.** 録音しておきましょう。

Kawa: Next, a few substitutions, as usual. "To buy" is **kaimasu.** Then, what about "I'll buy it," in the sense that you'll make sure the thing will always be available when necessary?

Goto: **Ka⌈tte okimasho⌉o.** 買っておきましょう。

Kawa: Next, "I'll make research on it." "To make research on something," **kenkyuu shimasu.**

Goto: **Ke⌈nkyuu shite okimasho⌉o.** 研究しておきましょう。

Kawa: One more. "I'll give him a phone call just in case." "To phone someone," **denwa o kakemasu.**

Goto: **De⌈nwa o ka⌉kete o⌈kimasho⌉o.** 電話をかけておきましょう。

Kawa: It's not absolutely necessary to call him now, but you'll do so because it may be better just in case something happens.

Goto: **De⌈nwa o ka⌉kete o⌈kimasho⌉o.** 電話をかけておきましょう。

♪ **Station Break** 〰〰〰〰〰〰〰〰〰〰〰〰〰〰〰〰〰〰〰〰〰〰〰

Kawa: Now, in the second half of this session, we'll discuss each dialogue. Listen to their conversation first.

◆ **Today's Conversation**

S: **Ni⌈ppo⌉n ni i⌈ru aida ni⌉ hi⌈to⌉tsu u⌈ta⌉ o o⌈boema⌉shita.**
日本にいる間にひとつ歌をおぼえました。

  I: **Ze˺hi u˻tatte kudasa˺i.**　ぜひ歌って下さい。

  S: **Mi˻na˺-san mo go˻zo˺nji no u˻ta˺ desu kara, i˻ssho ni utatte kudasa˺i.**
　　みなさんもご存じの歌ですから、いっしょに歌って下さい。

  I: **So˻o shimasho˺o. Ki˻nen ni˺ ro˻kuon shite okimasho˺o.**
　　そうしましょう。記念に録音しておきましょう。

Kawa: Next, you'll listen to its English version.

◆ Same Conversation in English

  S: I learned a song during my stay in Japan.

  I: Sing it for us, please.

  S: This is a song you all know, so please sing along with me.

  I: We will do that. I will record it as a reminder of today.

Kawa: Now each dialogue. Mr. Smith says, "I learned a song during my stay in Japan." This is almost like the first key sentence.

Goto: **Ni˻ppo˺n ni i˻ru aida ni˺ hi˻to˺tsu u˻ta˺ o o˻boema˺shita.**
　　日本にいる間にひとつ歌をおぼえました。

Kawa: "During my stay in Japan."

Goto: **Ni˻ppo˺n ni i˻ru aida ni.**　日本にいる間に

Kawa: **Aida ni** means "during" or "while." "I learned a song:"

Goto: **Hi˻to˺tsu u˻ta˺ o o˻boema˺shita.**　ひとつ歌をおぼえました。

Kawa: **Hitotsu** means "one." "I learned a song during my stay in Japan."

Goto: **Ni˻ppo˺n ni i˻ru aida ni˺ hi˻to˺tsu u˻ta˺ o o˻boema˺shita.**
　　日本にいる間にひとつ歌をおぼえました。

Kawa: "Good for you. Why don't you sing it for us?"

Goto: **Ze˺hi u˻tatte kudasa˺i.**　ぜひ歌って下さい。

Kawa: **Zehi** means "by all means." **Utatte kudasai**, "Please sing it for us."

Goto: **Ze˺hi u˻tatte kudasa˺i.**　ぜひ歌って下さい。

Kawa: Mr. Smith would like them to sing with him. "This is a song you all know, so please sing along with me."

Goto: **Mi˻na˺-san mo go˻zo˺nji no u˻ta˺ desu kara, i˻ssho ni utatte kudasa˺i.**
　　みなさんもご存じの歌ですから、いっしょに歌って下さい。

Kawa: "A song you all know."

Goto: **Mi˻na˺-san mo go˻zo˺nji no u˻ta˺.**　みなさんもご存じの歌

Kawa: **Mina-san**, "all of you;" **gozonji** means "know" and is very respectful. But this polite word is only for others. Never say **gozonji** for yourself. "It's a song you all know, so…."

Goto: **Mi⌈na⌉-san mo go⌈zo⌉nji no u⌈ta⌉ desu kara,**
みなさんもご存じの歌ですから、

Kawa: "Please sing along with me."

Goto: **I⌈ssho ni utatte kudasa⌉i.** いっしょに歌って下さい。

Kawa: **Issho ni,** "together." "This is a song you all know, so please sing along with me."

Goto: **Mi⌈na⌉-san mo go⌈zo⌉nji no u⌈ta⌉ desu kara, i⌈ssho ni utatte kudasa⌉i.**
みなさんもご存じの歌ですから、いっしょに歌って下さい。

Kawa: Both Mr. and Mrs. Ito agree. Mr. Ito says, "We will do that. I will record it as a reminder of today."

Goto: **So⌈o shimasho⌉o. Ki⌈nen ni⌉ ro⌈kuon shite okimasho⌉o.**
そうしましょう。記念に録音しておきましょう。

Kawa: This remark contains the second key sentence, **rokuon shite okimashoo**. **Soo shimashoo** at the beginning means "We'll do that."

Goto: **So⌈o shimasho⌉o.** そうしましょう。

Kawa: Mr. Ito would like to record this memorable occasion. "As a reminder" is **kinen ni**, so he says, "I will record it as a reminder of today."

Goto: **Ki⌈nen ni⌉ ro⌈kuon shite okimasho⌉o.**
記念に録音しておきましょう。

Kawa: **Kinen** means "commemoration." "I will record it," suggesting that they'll be able to recollect this memorable day in the future.

Goto: **Ro⌈kuon shite okimasho⌉o.** 録音しておきましょう。

Kawa: "I will record it as a reminder of today."

Goto: **Ki⌈nen ni⌉ ro⌈kuon shite okimasho⌉o.**
記念に録音しておきましょう。

Kawa: Let's now listen to the whole conversation again.

◆ **Today's Conversation**

S: **Ni⌈ppo⌉n ni i⌈ru aida ni⌉ hi⌈to⌉tsu u⌈ta⌉ o o⌈boema⌉shita.**
日本にいる間にひとつ歌をおぼえました。

I: **Ze⌉hi u⌈tatte kudasa⌉i.** ぜひ歌って下さい。

S: **Mi⌈na⌉-san mo go⌈zo⌉nji no u⌈ta⌉ desu kara, i⌈ssho ni utatte kudasa⌉i.**
みなさんもご存じの歌ですから、いっしょに歌って下さい。

I: **So⌈o shimasho⌉o. Ki⌈nen ni⌉ ro⌈kuon shite okimasho⌉o.**
そうしましょう。記念に録音しておきましょう。

Kawa: Next, as usual, you'll practice today's vocabulary. Please repeat aloud after Goto-san, who will say each word or phrase twice. First, "song."

Goto: U⌈ta⌉. 歌

Kawa: "To memorize."

Goto: O⌈boema⌉su. おぼえます。

Kawa: "To record."

Goto: Ro⌈kuon shima⌉su. 録音します。

Kawa: "By all means."

Goto: Ze⌉hi. ぜひ

Kawa: Now the key sentences again. This time, just listen to Goto-san. The first key sentence: "I learned various songs during my stay in Japan."

Goto: Ni⌈ppo⌉n ni i⌈ru aida ni⌉ i⌈roiro⌉ u⌈ta⌉ o o⌈boema⌉shita.
日本にいる間に、いろいろ歌をおぼえました。

Kawa: Next, the second key sentence: "I will record it."

Goto: Ro⌈kuon shite okimasho⌉o. 録音しておきましょう。

Kawa: Now, you'll listen to their conversation again.

◆ **Today's Conversation**

S: Ni⌈ppo⌉n ni i⌈ru aida ni⌉ hi⌈to⌉tsu u⌈ta⌉ o o⌈boema⌉shita.
日本にいる間にひとつ歌をおぼえました。

I: Ze⌉hi u⌈tatte kudasa⌉i. ぜひ歌って下さい。

S: Mi⌈na⌉-san mo go⌈zo⌉nji no u⌈ta⌉ desu kara, i⌈ssho ni utatte kudasa⌉i.
みなさんもご存じの歌ですから、いっしょに歌って下さい。

I: So⌈o shimasho⌉o. Ki⌈nen ni⌉ ro⌈kuon shite okimasho⌉o.
そうしましょう。記念に録音しておきましょう。

Notes

1. V-1 **aida ni** V-2

This pattern means "V-2 happens (or happened) while V-1 is (or was) in progress."

Ni⌈ppo⌉n ni iru a⌈ida⌉ ni u⌈ta⌉ o oboemashita. V-1 is i⌈ru and V-2 is o⌈boema⌉shita, so "He learned a song while he was staying in Japan." V-1 is in the present tense regardless of the tense of the main verb, V-2.

Ma˥tte iru aida ni de˥nwa o ka˥kete kimashita. ("I went to make a phone call—and came back—while we were waiting.")
Mi˥nna˥ ga ˥te˥rebi o ˥mi˥te iru aida ni ˥ryo˥ori o tsu˥kurimasho˥o. ("While everyone is watching TV, I'll cook.")

Because **ni** denotes a point in time, if you omit **ni** the meaning is changed to "While V-1 was in progress, V-2 was also in progress the whole time."

Go˥han o tabete iru aida ˥te˥rebi o mimashita. ("We watched TV throughout the meal.")

2. Mi˥na˥-san mo go˥zo˥nzi no u˥ta˥ desu.

Go˥zo˥nji no u˥ta˥ is an honorific equivalent of **shi˥tte iru uta** ("the song you know"). **Shi˥tte ima˥su** mean "I know," but its negative form is **shi˥rimase˥n** rather than **shi˥tte imase˥n**.

When you are talking to someone who is "superior" to you or to whom you wish to show respect, the conversation might go like this:

You: **Ko˥no uta˥ go˥zo˥nji desu ka.** (honorific form)
He: **E˥e, shi˥tte ima˥su. Or: I˥ie, shi˥rimase˥n.** (plain form)
A˥no uta˥ o shi˥tte ima˥su ka. (plain form)
You: **Ha˥i, zo˥njite orima˥su. Or: I˥ie, zo˥njimase˥n.** (humble form)

3. o˥boema˥su vs. o˥bo˥ete imasu

O˥boema˥su means the act of committing to one's memory, or "to learn;" "to memorize." To say, "I remember," in the sense of "I have it in my memory bank," you have to say, **o˥bo˥ete imasu**, not **o˥boema˥su**.

A: **Ki˥no˥o wa ka˥nji o i˥kutsu oboemashita ka.** ("How many Chinese characters did you learn yesterday?")
B: **Sa˥njuu oboemashita.** ("I learned 30.")
A: **I˥ma mi˥nna obo˥ete imasu ka.** ("Do you remember all of them now?")
B: **E˥e, ze˥nbu o˥bo˥ete iru to omoimasu.** ("Yes, I think I remember them all.")

Exercises

1. Making necessary changes, substitute the cue for the underlined phrase in the example.

Example: **Ni˥ppo˥n ni iru aida ni, i˥roiro uta˥ o o˥boema˥shita.**

1. ko˥toba˥ o o˥boe˥ru
2. ki˥ree na to˥koro˥ o ˥mi˥ru
3. o˥ishii mono˥ o ta˥be˥ru
4. hi˥to ni a˥u
5. ha˥nashi˥ o ki˥ku

2. Connect the two halves of the cue with aˈida ni.

Example: **Niˈppoˈn ni iru; iˈroiro utaˈ o oˈboemaˈshita.→Niˈppoˈn ni iru aida ni iˈroiro utaˈ o oˈboemaˈshita.**

1. **Kyoˈoto ni iru; iˈroiro otera o mimaˈshita**
2. **shoˈkuji o shite iru; Taˈnaka-san ga kimaˈshita**
3. **maˈtte iru; teˈgami o kakimashoˈo**
4. **miˈnnaˈ ga ˈteˈrebi o ˈmiˈte iru; soˈoji o shite kudsaˈi**
5. **oˈfuˈro ni haitte iru, deˈnwa ga kimaˈshita**

3. Form sentences ending in -te okimashoˈo.

Example: **roˈkuon suru→Roˈkuon shite okimashoˈo.**

1. **biˈiru o kau**
2. **juˈnbi suru**
3. **soˈoji suru**
4. **shaˈshin o toˈru**
5. **deˈnwa o kakeˈru**

4. Substitute the cue for the word underlined in the model phrase.

Model phrase: **Aˈto de kiˈkeru yoˈo ni**

1. **noˈmeˈru**
2. **tsuˈkaeru**
3. **koˈmaraˈnai**
4. **miˈrareˈru**
5. **aˈeˈru**

5. Substituting your answers from Exercises 3 and 4 for the phrases underlined in the model, write new dialogues.

Model: A: **Roˈkuon shite okimashoˈo ka.**
B: **Eˈe, aˈto de kiˈkeru yoˈo ni roˈkuon shite oˈite kudasai.**

6. Express the following in polite Japanese. Try to use polite forms wherever possible.

1. Do you know Mr. Smith?
2. Have you ever been to Kyoto?
3. Would you please record it as a reminder (of today)?
4. Has your husband come home?
5. Do you remember Mr. Itoo's phone number?
6. Would you please sing a song?

Answers

1. 1. Ni⌐ppo⌐n ni iru aida ni, i⌐roiro kotoba⌐ o o⌐boema⌐shita.
   2. Ni⌐ppo⌐n ni iru aida ni, i⌐roiro ki⌐ree na tokoro o mi⌐ma⌐shita.
   3. Ni⌐ppo⌐n ni iru aida ni, i⌐roiro oishii mono⌐ o ta⌐bema⌐shita.
   4. Ni⌐ppo⌐n ni iru aida ni, i⌐roiro hito ni aima⌐shita.
   5. Ni⌐ppo⌐n ni iru aida ni, i⌐roiro hanashi⌐ o ki⌐kima⌐shita.

2. 1. Kyo⌐to ni iru aida ni, i⌐roiro otera o mima⌐shita.
   2. Sho⌐kuji o shite iru aida⌐ ni, Ta⌐naka-san ga kima⌐shita.
   3. Ma⌐tte iru aida ni, te⌐gami o kakimasho⌐o.
   4. Mi⌐nna⌐ ga ⌐te⌐rebi o mite iru aida ni, so⌐oji o shite kudasa⌐i.
   5. O⌐furo ni ⌐ha⌐itte iru aida ni, de⌐nwa ga kima⌐shita.

3. 1. Bi⌐iru o ka⌐tte okimasho⌐o.
   2. Ju⌐nbi shite o⌐kimasho⌐o.
   3. So⌐oji shite okimasho⌐o.
   4. Sha⌐shin o to⌐tte okimashoo.
   5. De⌐nwa o ka⌐kete okimasho⌐o.

4. 1. A⌐to de no⌐me⌐ru yoo ni
   2. A⌐to de tsu⌐kaeru yo⌐o ni
   3. A⌐to de ko⌐mara⌐nai yoo ni
   4. A⌐to de mi⌐rare⌐ru yoo ni
   5. A⌐to de a⌐e⌐ru yoo ni

5. 1. A: Bi⌐iru o ka⌐tte okimasho⌐o ka.
      B: E⌐e, a⌐to de no⌐me⌐ru yoo ni ka⌐tte o⌐ite kudasai.
   2. A: Ju⌐nbi shite o⌐kimasho⌐o ka.
      B: E⌐e, a⌐to de tsu⌐kaeru yo⌐o ni ⌐ju⌐nbi shi⌐te o⌐ite kudasai.
   3. A: So⌐oji shite okimasho⌐o ka.
      B: E⌐e, a⌐to de ko⌐mara⌐nai yoo ni so⌐oji shite o⌐ite kudasai.
   4. A: Sha⌐shin o to⌐tte okimashoo ka.
      B: E⌐e, a⌐to de mi⌐rare⌐re yoo ni ⌐to⌐tte oite kudasai.
   5. A: De⌐nwa o ka⌐kete o⌐kimasho⌐o ka.
      B: E⌐e, a⌐to de a⌐e⌐ru yoo ni de⌐nwa o ka⌐kete oite kudasai.

6. 1. Su⌐misu-san o go⌐zo⌐nji desu ka.
   2. Kyo⌐oto ni i⌐rassha⌐tta koto ga a⌐rima⌐su ka.
   3. Ki⌐nen ni ro⌐kuon shite o⌐ite ku⌐dasaimase⌐n ka.
   4. Go⌐shu⌐jin wa o⌐kaeri ni narima⌐shita ka.
   5. I⌐too-san no denwaba⌐ngoo o o⌐bo⌐ete irasshaimasu ka.
   6. U⌐ta⌐ o u⌐tatte kudasaimase⌐n ka.